BOOKS BY SAME AUTHOR

1. Yona L (2012) *Financial Accounting for Executives MBA.* Author House Publisher UK – ISBN 978148178010

2. Yona L (2011) *International Finance for Developing countries.* Author House Publisher UK – ISBN 9781456781705

3. Yona L (2010) *Corporate Finance. Author House-* Publisher UK ISBN 9781456781705

4. Yona L (2008) *Financial Management Skills for Non- Finance Managers.* Learn and Share Publishers – ISBN 9987425127

# CONTEMPORARY ISSUES IN TAXATION

Lucky Yona

authorHOUSE

AuthorHouse™ UK
1663 Liberty Drive
Bloomington, IN 47403 USA
www.authorhouse.co.uk
Phone: 0800.197.4150

© 2018 Lucky Yona. All rights reserved.

No part of this book may be reproduced, stored in a retrieval system, or transmitted by any means without the written permission of the author.

Published by AuthorHouse 04/09/2018

ISBN: 978-1-5462-9109-1 (sc)
ISBN: 978-1-5462-9108-4 (e)

Print information available on the last page.

Any people depicted in stock imagery provided by Getty Images are models, and such images are being used for illustrative purposes only.
Certain stock imagery © Getty Images.

This book is printed on acid-free paper.

Because of the dynamic nature of the Internet, any web addresses or links contained in this book may have changed since publication and may no longer be valid. The views expressed in this work are solely those of the author and do not necessarily reflect the views of the publisher, and the publisher hereby disclaims any responsibility for them.

Contents

Preface vii

Chapter 1: Overview of Taxation 1
Chapter 2: Developing Tax Policies 19
Chapter 3: Tax Administration 31
Chapter 4: Tax Evasion and Tax Avoidance 41
Chapter 5: Tax Planning 57
Chapter 6: Tax Reforms 67
Chapter 7: Tax Incentives 79
Chapter 8: Investment Climate 95
Chapter 9: Tax Compliance 115
Chapter 10: Tax Harmonization 129
Chapter 11: Tax Investigation 141
Chapter 12: Widening the Tax Base 159
Chapter 13: Tax Exmption 171
Chapter 14: Foreign Debt 179
Chapter 15: Balance of Payments 195

Bibliography 207
About the Author 211

Preface to First Edition

This book is all about public finance and contemporary issues in Taxation. The book discusses about contemporary issues in Taxation that cater across all developing countries as well as it discusses the concept of public debts and balance of payments related issues that are critical for economic development of a country. Students undertaking their undergraduate studies, postgraduate and professional studies will find the book to be useful and full of knowledge in the various issues that affect taxation of their countries.

Dedicated

To My Sons Lucky Yona Jr and Timothy Lucky

1. OVERVIEW OF TAXATION

❑ **Topic Objectives**
The topic intends to equip students with general overview of concepts and theories of taxation

❑ **Coverage**
1.1 Introduction
1.2 Why Taxation is important
1.3 Tax classification
1.4 Tax Systems
1.5 Principles of Taxation
1.6 Overview of Taxation in Selected African Countries
Practice Questions

❑ **Learning Outcome**
At the end of this topic, students will have understood the role of taxation and rationale of paying taxes

CHAPTER 1
Overview of Taxation

1.1. INTRODUCTION

Taxation had existed since long time when kingdoms as a form of leadership and governance started in the history of human beings. Although the collection of taxes was not in the form of money as it is today, it existed in other forms of exchange that was prevailing at that time. During the era of barter trade, taxpayer paid commodities. In the times when silver and gold was the means of exchange taxpayers paid the same. Looking at the history of kingdoms across the world, we can see that king's collected goods, silver, gold and other items as head taxes from citizens. Even the Bible contains records of various kingdoms like Solomon kingdom where the Israelites had to pay taxes. It looks that not all tax collections were voluntary but enforced upon the taxpayers.

With this knowledge of taxation, we can also review various definitions of tax. One of the definitions is the one, which considers tax as a compulsory contribution to the government by corporate and none- corporate citizens to support government expenditure to meet the expenditures on public services. The corporate citizens include individual and corporations. This definition, therefore, gives an indication that taxation is not a voluntary action that taxpayers are expected to be willing to contribute their part of the income to the government. Tax is also chargeable on properties, commodities, and transactions. Jonathan (2006) argues that tax is among the means of public resources mobilization; therefore, designing a tax system should provide incentives for economic growth and increase revenue collection.

On the other side, we can say taxation is a voluntary and a compulsory contribution of money from individuals and corporate entity to the government to meet the public expenditure. This definition of tax gives a broader meaning by including the word voluntary, meaning that the government does not always force taxpayers to pay the taxes, but they may opt not to pay or pay the taxes. Literary it is true that they are free to pay taxes or not, but in essence, it cannot be voluntary when they consume the products. They are automatically forced to pay taxes when they consume goods and services of which taxes are chargeable to them.

1.2. WHY TAXATION IS IMPORTANT

The only major way in which governments can raise funds to support its public expenditures is through taxation. The question, which governments need to answer, is what does government spending mean? Government spending includes all expenditures, which is the provision of social services, maintenance of law and order; provide defense and other undertakings, which the private sector cannot provide.

Countries, which cannot raise enough funds through taxation, are likely to have difficulties in meeting the public expenditure. Most developing countries due to inability to correct enough taxes have experienced problems of funding their operations and development budgets and tend to rely on donors to support their budget. In Africa, for example, very few countries like Kenya, by 2009 had successfully managed to fund its budget by 100%, while Tanzania managed to fund its budget by only 65% and the rest was from donor funds.

Many countries use Taxation as a policy instrument to protect local industries. In this case, consumer of imported goods pays high taxes while local products produced by local industries enjoy preferential tax rates lower than the ones of imported goods. Charging high taxes on imported goods makes the prices of local products cheaper than imported ones. However, in the modern days where there are regional integrations such as the East Africa Community and tax harmonization within the member countries in the integration, taxation is used to protect the industries of the member states.

Governments can also use taxation as an instrument of discouraging certain habits, which are considered harmful to the public such as the use of tobacco, cigarettes, spirits, and alcohol by imposing high taxes on consumptions of these types of products. The major argument or question to this objective is this; why should the government put laws that prohibit the use of these products if they are harmful to the citizens? The answer to this question is that the government must raise enough revenue from various sources. At the same time, people have the freedom to make choices what products they should consume or not consume.

At the same time, the government uses taxation as an instrument of mobilizing and accumulating capital from the general public and concentrating the wealth to the use of governments in capital development projects and investments. The Government cannot spend all its funds in re-current expenditure, but part of the funds collected through taxation can be for development and investments such as the construction of infrastructures such as roads, dam construction, and power generation plant.

Another justification is on the basis of wealth distribution among citizens in the given society. Governments achieve this through taxing rich people and providing services to the majority of the public, consistent with progressive taxation where individuals with high income will pay higher taxes and those with income will pay less tax. On the other side, the government uses tax to help allocate the available resources in the country to bring development in those geographical areas, which are underdeveloped. As a strategy by a government to ensure even distribution of development in a country, more resources through taxation means will be given to such areas to support infrastructure development and economic projects.

1.3 TAX CLASSIFICATION

There are various types of tax classification, which are useful to understand the tax as used under various tax jurisdictions. These classifications of taxes can be done in a number of ways to help policy maker to come up with tax systems that are favorable to both government and taxpayers.

HEAD TAX

Tax levied on the existence of a taxpayer, such as a levy of a certain amount paid by all individuals over minor age. This is not so common in most tax jurisdictions. Countries like Tanzania, Kenya and Uganda during colonial regimes had head taxes levied on individual above 18 years.

INCOME TAX

The charge of the tax is on individual income or corporate income. The income tax on individual is termed as Pay as you earn (P.A.Y.E) although some countries have other types of taxes levied on individuals. Taxation on the corporation is levied on both residents and non-residents companies. Tax rate varies from among various tax jurisdictions. Some tax jurisdictions have the same rate of income taxes for all types of companies while others have different rate depending on the resident status of the company. Income taxes are progressive in nature simply because they are payable depending on the income level of the taxpayer. The principle applicable is that the higher the incomes pay more taxes and vice versa. In terms of compliance, governments do not experience much challenges in compliance by taxpayers.

COMMODITY TAXES

These taxes are payable based on commodities. As people consume the product they pay taxes without or with the knowledge that taxes is included in the price of the product. Example of commodity taxes includes the Value added tax and sales taxes. Commodities taxes are regressive taxes where people with less income have more pinch than the ones with higher income.

WEALTH TAXES

These are payable on the wealth of the taxpayer. This includes such tax as estate duty, property taxes and capital gains taxes. Depending on the tax administrative efficiency, some countries have tried to use these types of taxes to increase government revenue though some countries have abandoned estate duty. In Africa, Tanzania is one of those countries, which do not have estate duty tax. Tanzania abandoned estate duty because it was not efficient in terms of cost of collection as compared to the revenue collected.

USER TAX

These also differ from one tax jurisdiction to another. They are taxes levied for use of a facility such as toll for a bridge, fuel or road. Depending on the cost of administering these taxes various jurisdictions have different ways of charging these taxes to the public.

TARIFF

The tariff is a tax or duty usually imposed on imported goods to increase the price of such goods relative to domestic goods.

1.4. TAX SYSTEMS

Ever since kingdoms and the government have existed in the world, various tax systems have been put into use. Few of those systems that are still in use today include the progressive tax system and regressive tax systems, which also do support the principles of taxations.

PROGRESSIVE TAX SYSTEM

This type of tax system is workings on the principle of ability to pay. Individuals or corporate entity pays taxes based on the level of earnings. The higher the level of earnings, the higher the rate of taxes that has to be paid. This means that individuals and corporate entities earning higher income will have to pay taxes at higher rates and those with lower income have to pay lower taxes. Typical example of a progressive tax system is where government levies corporation taxes based on company's profitability though the tax rates could be the same but the amount paid at the end is higher based on the level of income.

Table 1.1 Corporate Taxes on Companies

Company Income (USD)	Corporation Tax rate	Amount of Tax (USD)
10,000,000	30%	3,000,000
20,000,000	30%	6,000,000
30,000,000	30%	9,000,000
40,000,000	30%	12,000,000

Source: Author 2017

By observing this table (Table 1.1), it is clear that corporate tax rate is the same for all companies irrespective of their profitability earnings whether higher profits or lower profits. However, the amount of tax payable is not the same for all companies as the amount of tax increases as the amount of profit increases. This system is in adherence to the equity principle of taxation discussed in the next sections. In terms of individual persons, progressive tax rates and the amount are not the same for all levels of income. The higher the income, the higher the tax rate and the amount paid. (Table 1.2)

Table 1.2. PAYE on Individual Incomes

Company Income (USD)	Tax Rate	Amount of Taxes (USD)
1,000	15	150
2,000	20	400
3,000	25	750
4,000	30	1200

Source: Author 2017

When depicted on the graph (Fig 1.1), it shows a graph moving upward from left to right showing that as income increases the amount of tax also increasing causing the graph moving from left to right in a progressive way.

Figure 1.1 PROGRESSIVE TAXES- Personal Taxes

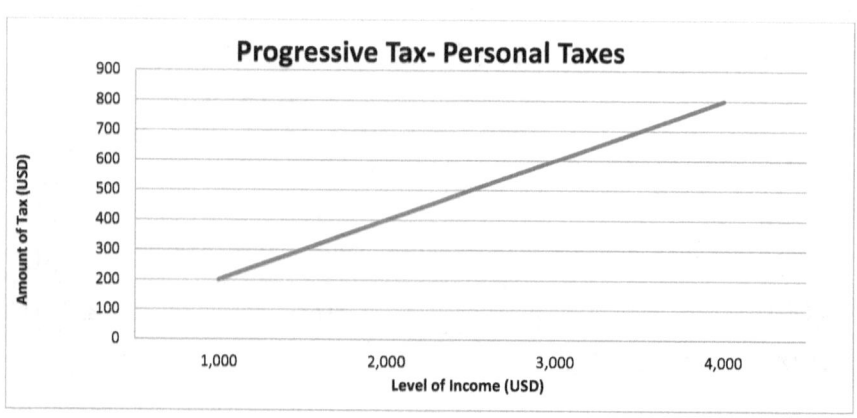

Source: Author 2017

PROPORTIONAL TAX SYSTEMS

With proportional tax systems, tax rate levied is the same for all levels of income. However, in the end the tax amount that is paid is progressive depending on the level of income. A typical example of proportional tax systems is the value added tax (VAT) or sales tax where the tax rates are fixed irrespective of the level of income of the taxpayer. The table below shows a typical example of fixed tax rates of 20% for all levels of income while the amount paid is higher as the level of income increases.

Table 1.3: Proportional Tax Rates

Company Income (USD)	Tax Rate	Amount of Taxes (USD)
1,000	20	150
2,000	20	400
3,000	20	750
4,000	20	1200

Source: Author 2017

REGRESSIVE TAX SYSTEMS

This tax system gives advantages to individuals and corporate entities that earn more to pay fewer amounts of taxes as compared to ones with lower taxes. However, the rate of taxes is the same to all groups of taxpayers but the amount paid is not the same. Example of regressive tax system is the sales taxes and VAT on goods. The tax amount that is paid by individuals who have less income increases more burdens to them as compared to individuals with higher income.

1.5 PRINCIPLES OF TAXATION

The canons of taxation are also termed as principles of taxation. These principles are expected to guide tax administration and collection in a given tax jurisdiction. Any tax system, which is likely to be effective, has to adopt these principles.

ABILITY TO PAY

Individuals and corporate entity should pay taxes according to their abilities. The higher the income, the higher the taxes that is payable. By applying this principle, even where countries apply the same rate of tax to all taxpayers, the amount will not be the same simply because that tax rate will be applicable to the amount of taxable income. This principle conforms to the proportional tax systems where the tax amount paid by taxpayers is proportional to their incomes.

SPREAD

Tax base of a country should be broad enough to incorporate a larger population of possible taxpayers and across many economic sectors in the country. This gives a wider opportunity for a country to raise more revenues and reduce the tax burden of few individuals. Where the spread is narrow it can be de-motivating and not fair to few individuals and groups that pay the taxes while majority are exempted in the tax net. Again, the narrow tax system might create in-efficiency in terms of boosting revenue collections.

CONVENIENCE

The convenience of tax system is achievable when payment of tax is more convenient to both tax payers and tax authorities when it comes to the collection of taxes. Convenience means the easiness of tax authorities to collect tax revenue without problem and minimizing costs. Convenience supports voluntary compliance by taxpayers. To the taxpayers it may mean the easiness of them paying taxes without cumbersome procedures.

EFFICIENCY

This principle requires that all tax systems put in place should enable the government to collect enough tax amounts with minimum costs and efforts. The cost of collecting the tax should be minimal as compared to the amount that the government can collect. Spending huge amount on cost of collection against less revenue is core thrust of this principle.

SIMPLICITY

Tax systems should be simple to administer by tax officials. Simplicity also includes the easiness of understanding the tax laws by both tax payers and tax administrator which can facilitate easy collection and voluntary compliance by taxpayers. A tax system with complex laws makes difficulty to interpret and understand which at the end it can encourage more tax evasion practices.

EQUITY

Tax system should enhance equity among taxpayers. All taxpayers should bear the tax burden in the society according to individual abilities. The tax burden should be borne by both individuals and corporate entities. Where there is no tax equity, only few people in a society bear the burden for tax payment responsibility.

1.6. TAXATION IN SELECTED AFRICAN COUNTRIES

All African countries have different history of colonization. These differences lead them to have slight differences in their tax systems and laws. Countries colonized by British government tend to resemble in their structure and laws with Britain laws with slight differences, while those countries which were under apartheid or French regimes have adopted their tax laws from South Africa or France systems. Immediately after their political independence these countries adopted tax systems and laws from their colonial masters. Even after independence, these countries have taken many years to reform their tax laws. The reforms undertaken tend to reflect what each country needs to meet its revenue requirements. Each of these countries have a wide range of taxes including income tax, value added tax, sales tax, transfer duty, capital gain and custom duties. The list is not exhaustive. However, a notable issue is that: each country levies are on basis, which suits the circumstances of a specific country.

With the ongoing regionalization movement in African countries into regional blocks like the East African Community, COMESA and SADC, taxation is now adopting the concept of tax harmonization which requires the harmonization of tax laws and tax rules in the regional blocks. Countries in the East African community integration has adopted harmonization in customs laws which forces all countries to apply same laws related to customs. Further Tax Harmonization initiatives in these blocks are still going on and will affect the taxations of businesses and individuals in these regional blocks. We will discuss tax harmonization in another chapter in this book.

PRACTICE QUESTIONS

Question 1

In view of the Principles of Taxation already discussed in this book, explain the common principles in the tax system of your country?

Question 2

Evaluate the impact and applicability of different classification of different taxation on the collection of tax revenues in your country.

Question 3

Identify the negative weaknesses of tax classification to both the government and the taxpayers in your country.

Question 4

Discuss how government can measure tax effectiveness.

Question 5

Discuss how African regional integrations influences taxation of countries in these integrations.

2. DEVELOPING TAX POLICIES

❑ **Topic Objectives**
The topic objectives are to provide basic knowledge to students on development of tax policies by governments

❑ **Coverage**
2.1. Introduction
2.2. Objectives of designing Tax Policy
2.3. Challenges in developing tax policies
2.4. Tax policy development in developing countries
2.5. Coping with the challenges in tax policy development
Practices

❑ **Learning Outcome**
At the end of this topic, students will have understood why tax policy plays a major role in a country development

CHAPTER 2

Developing Tax Policies

2.1. INTRODUCTION

One of the major factors that contribute to development of a country is the availability of good monetary and fiscal policies. The fiscal policies are the ones, which deal with taxes that the government can use to collect more revenues from the public. Since governments depends so much on taxes collected in the economy a need for designing proper tax policies that can easily facilitate revenue collection and achieve other objectives becomes important.

However, it is not an easy job to develop a tax policy as many factors can influence the design. Tax policy development may be shaped by number of factors including the specific political institutions, personal ideas and vested interest (Steinammo, 1993). In developing countries institutions interest and ideas are ones of the critical factors in shaping the tax policies. In actual fact it has never appeared that a country has a single tax structure that can address all tax objectives of a country.

On the other hand, the desire and need for increased public services and country economic development have also to be taken into consideration.

Developing tax policies requires governments to be aware of the impacts that are likely to arise as the result of the implementation of new policies. Tax policies can have both positive and negative impact to the effectiveness of revenue collection, performance of economic sectors as well as development of investments. If not well designed it is likely to increase the rate of tax evasion and avoidance.

An ideal tax system should be favorable to both parties; this means that it must bring a win-win situation to the government as well as to the taxpayers. It should support the government in raising revenues without discouraging taxpayers and productive economic activities. In designing tax policies and systems, governments should benchmark with other tax policies and systems in other countries especially in the regional blocks.

2.2. OBJECTIVES OF DEVELOPING TAX POLICY

Developing tax policy without proper objectives is likely not bringing any economic or social benefits to the government and its citizens. Tax policies are designed with specific objectives in mind. Although the primary purpose of designing tax policy is to help the government to collect taxes in order is to finance government expenditure, tax policies can also help the government to achieve other objectives. Therefore, it is important to take into consideration other objectives in designing the tax policies. These include the following tax objectives, among others:

a. Redistribution of income: This is done through the use of progressive rate structures whereby the imposition of high taxes on those with greater ability to pay. This reduces income inequality in the country.
b. Attract investment and increase revenue collection Tax Policies are put in place with the aim of attracting Investments both from within and outside the country (FDI) and therefore grow the country's revenue collections.
c. Influencing the Economy Taxes should also be used to influence the economy. Tax cuts should be used (1) to stimulate the economy by putting more money in taxpayers' pockets, and (2) to provide incentive for work and saving.
d. Equality-Achieving equality means that those with equal ability to pay taxes, all other things being equal, should pay the same tax.
e. Economic Efficiency- Efficiency implies that the damaging effects of tax policy should be kept to minimum.
f. Protection of local industries-Sometimes taxes are imposed to protect domestic industries from foreign competition. A high import duty on a product may reduce the import of a commodity and enable domestic producers to produce the commodity at

home. Similarly, a subsidy on export of a particular product can increase its competitiveness in the world market by reducing its price and raising its export.

2.3. TAX POLICY DEVELOPMENT IN DEVELOPING COUNTRIES

Developing tax policies follows same acceptable principles of taxation. However, tax policy development in developing countries may show different directions subject to new trends in regional blocks and internationalization in the global business arena. In regional blocks such as the East African Countries the need to harmonize the taxes among member countries might has influenced the tax policies and tax structures. At the same time, the move of the Multinational corporations to invest in developing countries poses a challenge of tax evasion by these companies hence a need of coming up with different tax policies. The following trends have emerged resulting to different approaches to tax policy developments;

1. Transfer Pricing Developments. With the influx of multinational companies, tax laws are now imbedded with strong anti-avoidance rules to tackle revenue loss through non-arm length transactions
2. Increase in Double Taxation Agreements so as to increase investment between countries. In some instances, this has caused some countries to be

exploited by companies who use the agreements to evade taxes.
3. Regional Integration (EAC, COMESA). The concept of tax harmonization is becoming important in all regional blocks with major aim of designing tax policies aimed at boosting cross border trade
4. Multinational Corporations moving to different countries are demanding for Increase in Tax Incentives, such as tax holidays and tax rebates. These have increasingly grown in developing countries in a bid to boost investment.
5. Technological advancement (Automation of tax systems, electronic fiscal devices)
6. Increased public awareness and sensitization of the public on the use of automated tax systems.

2.4. CHALLENGES IN DEVELOPING AND IMPLEMENTING TAX POLICIES

There is a trend going on now on regionalization of countries across the globe. Example of regional integration is the East Africa community (EAC), Southern African Developed Countries (SADC) and the European countries (EU). These regional integrations demand tax harmonization, which at the end requires developing tax policies for the whole region and not just for one country. Since each of the countries in the regionalization have their own policies, developing tax policies that can suit the needs of all countries at the same time will face many challenges, which could include the political differences between the pioneers who are supposed to engineer the system hence slowing the implementation of tax policies.

Another critical challenge on tax policy development is the increased pressure to reduce various taxes by various groups. Pressure on reduction of personal taxation, VAT, corporate taxes as well as import and export taxes are the common trend in the global economies. These pressures are forcing individual countries to re-think on their taxes in order to address these challenges. On the other side increased technological innovation and digitized business transactions are causing a greater need for revised tax policies.

The differences in currencies among countries pose a challenge in designing tax policies as well as the economic strength of each member countries. Other challenges are the loopholes in tax laws which are exploited and lead to tax avoidance and hence this causes loss of revenue. On the other side lack of expertise and capacity to implement complex agreements hence exploitation by multi nationals

1. Countries want to maintain the sanctity of their sovereignty and are therefore rigid and unwilling to adopt new policies.
2. Political will in most developing countries. Tax policies implementation is occasionally halted by some political figures for selfish reasons
3. Cyber insecurity increases costs of administration and compliance.

4. Tax Incentives encourage investment but at the same time cause revenue loss. It is difficult to obtain a balance
5. Poor communication strategies by revenue authorities to the population
6. Rampant corruption that has caused high taxes evasion

2.5. COPING WITH THE CHALLENGES IN TAX POLICY DEVELOPMENT

The challenges of designing tax policies might not be the same across the whole world. Developed countries might have fewer challenges as compared to developing countries like the ones in Sub-Saharan African Countries. The importance of benchmarking the tax laws or the use of model tax laws like the OECD model on double taxation (DTA) might help to come up with a robust regime.

Another issue is to address the inadequate capacity of tax drafting in developing countries by building the country capacity in tax laws drafting as well as acquiring expertise in tax law and interpretation and interpretations of tax agreements implementation. Embracing the need to incorporate taxation of businesses in digitized economies is critical for developing countries as they try to review their tax policies. Developed countries are ahead in designing tax policies and structures that copes with the technology advancement.

Fighting corruption at higher level would positively

influence various policies decisions including the fiscal policies. Higher level of corruption lowers the capacity of government officials to develop sound tax policies as they can only develop and implement those policies which favors the corrupt individuals.

PRACTICE QUESTIONS

Question 1

Evaluate the tax policy development in your country. What weaknesses are inevitable?

Question 2

Discuss what are likely to be the main objectives for tax policy development in any tax jurisdiction.

Question 3

What are the main challenges and limitations in designing and implementing the tax policies?

Question 4

What are the benefits for designing tax policies in any tax Jurisdiction?

3. TAX ADMINISTRATION

❑ **Topic Objectives**
The topic intends to introduce students to issues related to tax administration

❑ **Coverage**
3.1 Introduction
3.2 Pillars of Tax Administration
3.3 Regulatory Framework
3.4 Organization Structure of Tax Administration
3.5 Laws regarding tax administration
3.6 Factors enhancing tax administration
Practice Questions

❑ **Learning Outcome**
At the end of this chapter, students should be able to understand what tax administration. Student will also understand role of tax administration in enhancing government revenue collect.

CHAPTER 3

Tax Administration

3.1. INTRODUCTION

Tax administration involves all issues that are pertinent for effective tax revenue collection in a given country. Tax administration may involve the administration of tax laws relating to specific taxes, undertaking all management functions in order to enhance effective tax collections on behalf of the government in power.

The design of Tax administration system should be in accordance to the overall purpose, scope and objectives of tax policy (Shome, 2004). The revenue authorities, or a specific department under the ministry of finance can do tax administration in a given country. Common practices in most African countries have moved away from the practice of tax administration by a treasury department of the ministry of finance to established revenue authorities.

These independent institutions have their own organizational structures that administer various tax laws as per established government act. Some of the countries that have adopted this approach of having a semi- autonomy Revenue Authority in Africa are countries like Kenya (Kenya Revenue Authority (KRA)), Tanzania (Tanzania Revenue Authority (TRA)), Uganda (Uganda Revenue Authority, (URA)), Malawi (Malawi Revenue Authority(MRA)), Zimbabwe (Zimbabwe Revenue Authority (ZIMRA)) and many other African Countries.

3.2 FUNCTIONS OF TAX ADMINISTRATION

Tax administration involves a number of functions that the revenue authority or treasury department has to undertake in order to ensure that the government is able to meet the tax objectives. The following are the main functions of tax administration

1. Administering various tax laws in a tax jurisdiction.
2. Collection of taxes from taxpayers.
3. Tax education to taxpayers in order to create awareness of the importance of taxes to the government.
4. Administering the procedure for tax collections on behalf of the government.
5. Capacity building for tax officials in order to enhance proper and effective tax collections.
6. Ensuring that there is proper mechanism for handling taxpayer's complaints and addressing them in order to ensure taxpayers continue complying with tax laws.

7. Management and supervision of all staff in the tax authority.
8. Management of assets for the tax authority or treasury department.

3.3 REGULATORY FRAMEWORK

The regulatory framework comprises of tax laws, regulations and procedures that govern tax assessment, tax collection and penalties to non-compliance of tax laws within a tax jurisdiction. Countries have the sole rights to have their own tax laws that govern tax administration without being interfered by another country. It is only in case where there is agreement between one country and another where the sovereignty on tax laws design will not exist. Typical example of such situation is when there are double taxation agreements between two countries or more and in such cases where there is regional tax harmonization, where tax laws become the same.

3.4 ORGANIZATION STRUCTURES FOR TAX ADMINISTRATION

In order to enhance tax administration, governments across the world do structure their tax authorities or revenue department in such a way that tax collection and administration is more efficient and effective. The organization structure of tax or revenue authorities in most countries operate around the major types of taxes that exist in the specific tax jurisdiction. Most countries have formed semi-autonomous tax authorities that operate independently from the ministry of finance. These tax authorities have different departments to cater for different types of taxes such as the income tax department; customs and value added taxes departments and commissioners head these departments.

In a recent move during this decade, most revenue or tax authorities have created specific departments for large taxpayers or corporate taxpayers. Examples of such authorities are, the Tanzania Revenue Authority (TRA), Kenya Revenue Authority (KRA) and Uganda Revenue Authority (URA) in East Africa.

3.5 LAWS REGARDING TAX ADMINISTRATION

Most laws that govern tax collection and administration are passed by the parliament and are made laws by the act of parliament. The acts can change over time when the need to do so arises. These laws are there to administer various taxes that are available in any given country. Some of the common laws that in most countries are for tax administration include

(a) Value Added Tax
(b) Income tax
(c) Customs tariffs
(d) Imports duty

(e) Excise Duty
(f) Estate duty
(g) Property taxes

3.6 CHALLENGES OF TAX ADMINISTRATION

Tax administration is full of challenges that can impair all efforts of tax collection by the revenue authority. If these challenges are not addressed sometimes, tax collection function cannot achieve its objectives. The challenges of tax authorities vary from one country to another. Kitlya (2011) and Shome (2004) identified a number of challenges to tax administration that various revenue authorities experience.

1. Political interference- where revenue authorities are interfered in decision making as regard to issues related to tax exemptions and curbing tax evaders.
2. Inadequate numbers of staff to manage tax collection, investigation and auditing supervision for the whole country. Most countries have huge number of taxpayers across the whole country and most income might go untaxed.
3. Insufficient appropriate modern technology that can cope with current economic environment
4. Corrupt tax officials give big challenges to both taxpayers and tax authorities. On the side of tax

authorities, it gives wrong image to the taxpayers in regard to the integrity of the authorities.
5. Taxpayers view tax officials as enemies and it has eroded the morality to pay taxes.
6. Complexity of tax laws that are difficult to understand and interpret, poses challenges to tax authority's staff.
7. Changing of staff mindset and integrity is a challenge that tax authorities have to address in order to cope up with corruption and irresponsibility.

3.7 FACTORS THAT CAN ENHANCE TAX ADMINISTRATION

In order to enhance tax administration, tax authorities can use various strategies. Kitlya (2011) argued about the management commitment to tax administration, need for political will and use of technical assistance from developed countries as strategies to enhance tax administration. Other factors that can bring success to tax administration include government support and financial support from the donor community, proper organization structures that promote good management of staff in the whole process of tax collections and existence of tax laws and regulations that are easy to interpret, understand and implement.

Tax authorities need to use appropriate modern technology that can enhance e- tax and e-Filling of tax returns; which can help in coping with the challenges of modern businesses. Tax authorities need to address the problem of Inadequate numbers of staff that are involved in tax collection, investigation and auditing supervision by making strategies on recruitment of staff from private sectors as well as from public training institutions.

PRACTICE QUESTIONS

Questions 1

Why Tax Administration is important for economic development of a country?

Question 2

What are the typical challenges that the revenue/tax authority in your country experience in tax administration?

Questions 3

What are the major functions that relate to tax administration?

Question 4

Discuss the key pillars of tax administration in the context of African Countries.

4. TAX EVASION AND TAX AVOIDANCE

❏ **Topic Objectives**
Introduce students and taxpayers to concepts of Tax evasion and tax avoidance.

❏ **Coverage**
4.1. Definition
4.2. Similarities between tax evasion and tax avoidance
4.3. Major causes of tax evasion and avoidances
4.4. Combating tax evasion and avoidance Practices
4.5. Challenges in combating tax evasion and avoidance
4.6. Weakness in the regulatory framework
4.7. Informal Sector and tax evasion
Practice Questions

❏ **Learning Outcome**
Students should be able to differentiate between tax evasion and avoidance and understand their causes and appropriate strategies to minimize or eliminate them.

CHAPTER 4

Tax Evasion and Tax Avoidance

4.1. DEFINITION

Tax evasion is a deliberate action by the taxpayer whether corporate or individual of designing the business transactions in such a way that one eliminates or reduces the tax liability while contravening the existing tax laws of the country. This practice gives a room to reduce or eliminate completely any tax obligation. Since this practice involves contravening the tax laws is illegal and it is punishable under tax laws.

Farayole (1987) defines tax evasion as the fraudulent, dishonest, intentional distortion or concealment of figures with the intention of payment of or reducing the amount of tax otherwise payable. Tax evasion is common in all over the world though some countries have severe punishments imposed on those who practice it. There are few cases of tax evasion documented but already we know that countries like china and Singapore have severe punishment to those who practice it. Therefore, it is not advisable for one to practice such actions because there are higher penalties attached to it.

Tax avoidance on the other side is a practice by corporate or individual taxpayers to reduce or eliminate tax obligations without breaking the tax laws of a country by looking at the loopholes or weaknesses of the present tax laws of the country (Mponguliana, 2005). This practice is a legal and therefore not punishable under tax laws. Ani (1978) describes tax avoidance as a trick or manipulation of tax laws in order to evade payment of tax. In this case the taxpayer knowing what the laws says, the taxpayer structures the business transactions in such a way that he less or no tax is paid. Tax avoidance practices happen when actions are taken to minimize tax while operating within the ambit of the law but contravening the object and spirit of the law.

4.2 SIMILARITIES AND DIFFERENCES

These two terms have the same objectives, which involve arrangement of business transaction with the aim of eliminating or minimizing the tax liability. If these practices are left to continue without any government intervention strategy, the government will not achieve maximum revenue from taxes.

The difference of these concepts is on the methods used to achieve their objectives. One uses the illegal means (Tax Evasion) and other is using legal means (Tax avoidance). While tax evasion is illegal and punishable, tax avoidance is not punishable. However, under government perspective both of them are not health and supportive to government efforts of raising revenue to meet public expenditure. The magnitude of the impact to government revenue of these practices will differ from one country to another due to strategies applied by an individual country. Where there are strong and effective strategies possibilities of lower impact is high. Each year governments lose a significant amount of money through these practices though one is not punishable and the other is punishable under the laws.

Tax evasion and avoidances impairs government efforts of raising funds to meet its public expenditure such as provision of health services, education and security services to the public hence a need to design strategies to combat these activities becomes critical.

4.3. MAJOR CAUSES OF TAX EVASION AND AVOIDANCE

The following factors are the major causes of tax evasion and avoidances in most countries. Various studies by different scholars (Mponguliana, 2005, Kiabel & Nwokah, 2011; Cobham, 2005) have identified variety of major causes of tax evasion. They apply in both cases of evasion and avoidance but some of them are so specific that is why it is important to group them as follows:

a. High tax rates

High tax rates create a desire for evasion. High tax rates de-motivate taxpayers to pay taxes and any tax evasion loophole available becomes attractive.

b. Misappropriation of Government funds
Where taxpayers are not happy or contented with how the government use their money. The public expect a quid pro-quo relationship between what they are paying and what they receive in terms of services from the government. Although the governments do not expect such relationship, taxpayers are much concerned such that if they do not see that relationship they seek ways of evading taxes. The taxpayers' expectations are not met therefore they end up evading tax.

c. Unfair tax collection
There exists unfairness in tax collection caused by discriminatory collection of taxes through weaknesses in the tax administration).

d. High levels of corruption
Existence of high level of corruption in the tax administration can cause collusion between taxpayers and tax officials helping individual or corporate entity to evade taxes

e. Political interference
Political interference for instance where a lot of tax waiver given to individuals or corporation on the discretion of tax officials or minister.

f. Absence of Tax paying culture
   Lack of tax- paying culture among citizens can cause tax evasion. This is problem which need to addressed by sensitization program to all levels of taxpayers

g. Gaps or loopholes in the law cause tax avoidance
   Any loophole or gaps in the tax laws can help individuals or corporate entity to evade taxes as payment of taxation is not a moral obligation.

h. Low remuneration to tax officials
   Tax officials responsible for tax administration and collection are paid low salaries and this results to lack of motivation to work which in returns leads to desire to aid people who to evade or avoid taxes.

i. Lack of motivation to pay tax – taxpayers do not see the advantages as there is always lack of a direct relationship between tax paid and the accruing benefits

j. Lack of control in tax administration – control mechanisms not in place, loopholes in the system, weaknesses in tax law, complex tax administration makes it difficult for tax payers to comply; excessive tax rates

k. Corruption by tax officials – they facilitate tax avoidance and evasion

l. Low prospect of detection and punishment of tax evaders

m. Lack of proper taxation policy for the informal sector

n. Inherent culture not to pay tax – low tax morality

4.4. COMMON EVIDENCE OF TAX EVASION AND AVOIDANCES PRACTICES

In order to combat tax evasion, it is important to have a deeper understanding of the causes and the evidence of tax evasion practices in the country. The understanding is important as it helps to design proper strategies to address the problems. Kiabel & Nwokah (2011) argues that tax evasion is achievable through various intentional activities such as failure to pay taxes, failure to submit returns and omission or misstatement of items from returns. Other intentional activities include claiming relief (in Personal Income Tax), for example, of children that do not exist, understating income, documenting fictitious transactions, overstating expenses and failure to answer queries during a tax audit exercises.

There are number of lessons that are learnt from tax experts of different countries as far as tax evasion is concerned. The following are common practices of tax evasion across countries:

a. Some taxpayers keep two sets of books of accounts; this is common among the businessperson across most of parties in the world. One set for the purpose showing the true performance of the business and the other to falsify the actual performance of the business to avoid paying any statutory obligation or tax liability
b. Optional receipting-This happens where business people give options to their customers to whether they should give them receipts or not give them receipts. In case customers do not get the receipts then the VAT is not chargeable on the sales.
c. False accounting and submission of factious documents
d. Where non-deductible expenses are treated as deductible expenses. A typical example of such cases happens where capital expenditure are treated as allowable expenses for tax purposes. Most tax laws do not allow such expenditure as revenue expenditure
e. Where there are no records kept for business transactions or there is poor record keeping, the room for tax evasion is high
f. High rate of smuggling activities in a country is an indicator for tax evasion. Not all smuggling activities follow normal channels of transacting business and therefore capturing of information for such business for tax purposes becomes difficult.

g. When there is high rate of under-declaration of incomes by big business enterprises is an indicator of tax evasion practices
h. The level of tax contribution to GDP of a country can indicate the level of evasion and avoidance in a country. Where there is low tax GDP ratio this can indicate high level of evasion and avoidance.
i. Non-submission of tax returns by taxpayer indicates high possibility of tax evasion practices.
j. Temporary avoidance, these are tax delays, which are not illegal. The taxpayer here frustrates attempts to collect tax by using judicial means i.e. delays in courts of law.
k. Where there are more claims by taxpayers of tax deductions and benefits which they are not entitled such as unlawful claims and non-payment of taxes collected on the behalf of the government. This is a common practice by employers deducting taxes from employees and not submitting to the revenue department.
l. Shifting of tax liabilities e.g. where there are two persons paying tax (for instance a company and an individual)
m. Use of off-shore companies where incomes are transferred to those companies
n. Invoicing splitting into many taxpayers
o. Use of tax exemptions to evade taxes

4.5. COMBATING TAX AVOIDANCE AND EVASION

All strategies to combat tax avoidance and evasion practice in the country should aim at eliminating or reducing tax losses to the government. Governments across the globe have been using some of these strategies;

1. Making provisions in law that impose obligations to taxpayers to file tax returns of income and chargeability to tax
2. Making provisions in law that empower the commissioners /director of revenue authorities or departments to examine the books of accounts of the taxpayers
3. Making provisions in the law that give powers to commissioner/directors of income taxes to counteract the avoidance or evasion transactions by making them void and illegal for tax purposes
4. Making provisions in the law that aim at preventing the use of trusts as conduit pipes or devices for accumulating capital
5. Ensuring that restructuring of tax laws and system is an ongoing process and not just a single event. This means that constant review of tax laws and regulations is important in deterring tax avoidances and evasion practices.
6. Computerization of the tax systems helps to strengthen the tax administration. Many countries

have now computerized their customs system by using for example E-tax and ASYCUDA package software
7. Tax education can help taxpayers to understand the importance of paying taxes as citizens hence reduce the element of evasion and avoidance. This is achievable through education and sensitization programs for employees and the citizens. By conducting trainings, seminars, workshops and use of media, taxpayers and tax officials can understand their responsibilities and be able to comply to tax laws requirements.

4.6. CHALLENGES OF COMBATING TAX EVASION AND AVOIDANCES

Fighting tax evasion and avoidance by government is an important aspect in enhancing government revenues. If these practices are un-attended, the government is likely to collect fewer amounts from taxes, which at the end its lowers the capacity to finance most of the public expenditures. Challenges experienced by most countries do not vary so much though the degree of variation can be influenced by country uniqueness and the surrounding economic and legal factors. However, these factors are common challenges in their efforts to combat tax evasion practice:

a. Political interference
b. Inadequate man power

c. High level of corruption in tax administration
d. Inadequate and ambiguous tax laws, which are difficult for interpretation and understanding
e. Poor enforcement methods of collecting tax
f. The data collected is not enough (it is inadequate)
g. Informal businesses are not registered and may have incomplete records or the do not have records at all and mix personal expenditure with business.
h. Lack of technical competencies of the revenue departments/authority staff
i. Lack of proper knowledge regarding taxation by the citizens
j. Inadequate or improper information technology
k. Lack of proper statics and trend analysis regarding taxation payments
l. Corruption by the authority employees
m. Lack of motivation by authority Employees
n. Weaknesses in the regulatory framework that impair government efforts in combating tax evasion practices, caused by weak laws, outdated laws, Poor enforcement methods and poor collection methods
o. Lack of national database –regulatory authorities lack details of persons liable to tax, rental income not known to the tax authorities, various govt agencies do not share information
p. Inadequate tax education – stakeholders not educated enough, understand importance of paying tax, consequences of tax avoidance and evasion

4.7. INFORMAL SECTOR CONTRIBUTION AND TAX EVASION

It is quite interesting for taxation students to undertake a study where possible in order to be able to understand ways of estimating and evaluating government tax losses from the shadow economy. The shadow economy or informal sector comprises of all economic activities, which are the tax collection mechanism is not capable of capturing tax from such sources. The range of this activities include activities like those of income from unregistered businesses, under declared profits of registered businesses and profits from criminal activities to work performed off the books. Where the shadow economy is large and government strategies to collect revenue from these sectors are not there or weak, the government is likely to obtain less income from tax revenue.

In most developing countries especially in African countries, the informal sector is large enough but the tax nets are too narrow to capture tax revenues for the governments. There are many types of businesses which are potential for tax revenues both in urban and rural areas but the tax law does not provide for tax net for such business. We can site few of these types of business to include among many the renovations, restaurants, alcoholic beverages, vehicle maintenances, food and non-alcoholic beverages business.

In some countries, there are other activities beyond the underground economy, which constitute major avenues for tax losses. Tax losses arising from non-tax productive activities such as unjustified claims for tax credits and input tax rebates are typical examples of those avenues. Other avenues are illegal activities that funnel into underground networks which causes a significant loss of money that would normally go into the legal economy and provide tax revenues for the government.

PRACTICE QUESTIONS

Question 1

Discuss in detail the main causes of tax evasion and avoidance in your country.

Question 2

What is the difference between tax evasion and tax avoidance? Explain their similarities and differences.

Question 3

What are the evidences that show the existence of tax evasion and practices in your country?

Question 4

What strategies can your country apply in combating tax evasion and avoidance practices?

Question 5

What weaknesses are there in regulatory framework in your country that impairs government efforts in combating tax evasion and avoidances practices?

5. TAX PLANNING

❑ Topic Objectives-
The topic intends to introduce students to the concept of tax planning and its relevance to modern business organizations

❑ Coverage
5.1. Introduction
5.2. Perquisites of tax planning
5.3. Avenues for Tax Planning
5.4. Factors for enhancing tax planning
5.5. Challenges of Tax Planning
Practice Questions

❑ Learning Outcomes
At the end of the topic, students should be able to undertake tax-planning projects.

CHAPTER 5

Tax Planning

5.1. INTRODUCTION

The concept of tax planning has not attracted so much attention to managers of business especially for those who had no opportunity to study taxation in their life. However, in the course of doing business managers find themselves in challenging situation where they are required to ensuring that their companies comply with tax laws where their businesses operate. It is not only issue of compliance, which creates a challenge, but also the issue of maximizing the profits after taxes. Company's managers are eager to know how they can minimize their tax liability and pay less taxes without contravening the tax laws, hence a need for tax planning.

Tax planning is a pre-planned arrangement where a company can structure its business transaction in order to minimize the tax liability without contravening tax laws. Tax planning is not illegal and is not punishable. In order to achieve its objectives, Tax planning uses tax avoidance techniques. Tax planning is related to tax avoidance and not tax evasion. In Tax planning, we use all techniques that tax avoidance use without contravening the laws and tax statutes. The objective of tax planning is to minimize or eliminate tax liability. Tax planning is a continuous process, which begins at company formation stage and continues from time to time taking into consideration of various changes of tax laws from time to time.

5.2 PRELIQUISITIES OF TAX PLANNING

Tax planning exercise is not an easy an easy assignment to accomplish. Several factors have to be considered in order to achieve maximum benefit from the planning exercise. Successful tax planning depends on number of factors, which include the followings:

1. Understanding the existing tax laws and other statutes of the country where the business is operating. Ignorance of tax laws and inability to interpret the laws properly impairs the business to arrange its business transactions in such a way that the company can benefit from tax loopholes.
2. Understanding the nature of the business and what laws give advantages for tax avoidance purposes. Tax income, for example differs if you are registering as a sole proprietor, partnership or a company. There are also exemptions given to taxpayer, depending on the nature of business registration.

3. Consulting, Tax Expatriates
   Tax planning requires high knowledge and experience on tax laws. Since most managers do not have such knowledge, tax affairs planning might need assistance from tax professionals. The use of tax expatriates is highly recommended for successfully tax planning exercise.
4. Need to Benchmark with other companies in the same businesses and industry. Learning from other companies could be useful as a tax-planning exercise is going on.
5. Tax planning has to be done from the initial stage of the business registration.

5.3 AVENUE FOR TAX PLANNING

Tax planning must be considered as a process and not just a one-time event and therefore it is important to do it as a continuous process from the inception of the business. Tax planning should be done from the time when the business entity is registered for the first time and continue throughout the lifetime of the entity. This can give tax advantages to the business organization. All individual engaged in the tax planning process must take into consideration the following key issues

   a. Being up-to-date with all the tax changes taking place from period to period. Tax laws keep changing from year to year and these changes may have

impact on allowable expenses hence deny the opportunity to avoid taxes.
b. Looking at all loopholes in the tax regimes where there are possibilities of avoiding tax
c. Looking at the tax exemption regimes existing in the country such as VAT, Income tax and Export Promotion Zones taxes.
d. Looking at tax incentives options available in the tax regime of a country such as the ones available under export processing zones and investment center

5.4. FACTORS FOR ENHANCING TAX PLANNING

Despite the fact that tax planning is an art that requires proper skills of the taxpayers, its effectiveness depends on other factors that require proper planning. Companies need to keep proper set of books of accounts to allow proper assessments of its tax obligations from time to time. On the other side it is also important for companies to employ qualified accountants who are conversant with the tax laws to enhance tax planning of their organization. In addition to this companies may employ consultants on tax planning

1. Keeping proper books of accounts
2. Employing qualified accountants to advise tax payers
3. Generally educating the public on taxation matters

4. Reduction of corruption
5. Simplifying tax laws, regulations and procedures
6. Making proposals for the relaxation of tax laws
7. Educate taxpayers on the importance of tax planning
8. Involve tax consultants on tax planning

5.5 CHALLENGES OF TAX PLANNING

Tax planning exercise is not always easy and smooth. Various challenges are likely to force the organization as it plans its tax affairs to minimize tax liability. These challenges are likely to face companies in their tax planning

1. Ignorance of tax laws- Tax laws are dynamic and volatile. From time to time governments tend to review their tax laws such that ignorance of the changes in tax laws might cause companies to plan their tax affairs using old laws hence that the company might come up with wrong calculations of tax figures
2. Complexity of the tax laws, which becomes difficult to understand and interpret by company tax officials might lead to under-estimating the tax liability of over-estimate the tax liability.
3. Lack of knowledge and experience on tax planning- Most companies they have challenges of having qualified and experienced staff as far as tax planning is concerned

4. Corruption in tax administration- The corruption in tax administration can be a stumbling block where tax official denies taxpayers with the opportunity of using tax experts to plan their tax matters and instating on the use of revenue officers to do the work
5. Volatility of the tax laws- One of the most challenging issues in tax planning is the volatility of the tax laws in a given country. Tax laws keep changing from time to time such that it becomes difficult to plan and forecast tax avoidance avenues.
6. Strict tax laws, which do not leave loopholes for avoidance or evasion creates no room for tax planning to taxpayers.
7. Low level of education by taxpayers denies them the opportunity to take advantages of the loopholes in tax laws as well as taking advantages of using the tax experts. Ignorant taxpayers do not have any knowledge in tax

PRACTICE QUESTIONS

Question 1

Select a business of your choice in your own country. This business can be a new business or ongoing business. As a tax expert, explore on how you can help this company to plan its tax affairs in the coming financial year without contravening the laws of your country. Which assumptions and factors will you consider as you do tax planning?

Question 2

What loopholes in the tax laws of your country still are giving room for effective tax planning for business organizations? Site few of these laws and explain how you can use them for tax planning without contravening the law.

Question 3

Discuss the factors for enhancing tax planning in your country.

Question 4

What is the difference between tax planning and Tax Avoidance?

Question 5

Discuss what are likely to be the main challenges of tax planning to the corporate taxpayers in your country.

6. TAX REFORMS

❏ Topic Objectives
This topic is designed to equip students with the knowledge of tax planning for an organization

❏ Coverage
6.1. Introductions
6.2. Key Objectives of tax reforms
6.3. Guiding Principles of tax reforms
6.4. Avenues for tax reforms
6.5. Trends and Emerging issues in Tax reforms.
6.6 Challenges in Tax reforms
Practice Questions

❏ Learning Outcome
At the end of the topic students should be to advise business organizations on undertaking tax planning exercises. Students should be able to demonstrate the purpose of tax planning implication of non-adherence and its relationship with other parts of the organization.

CHAPTER 6

Tax Reforms

6.1 INTRODUCTION

Tax reforms are the process of changing the way taxes are collected or managed by the government. Therefore, as governments continue discovering weaknesses and loopholes in their tax systems, laws, policies, and systems that enhance more tax avoidance and tax evasion they embark to tax reforms in order to strengthen the systems and processes. Devas (2001) argues that tax reforms should help to increase government revenues, curb corruption and therefore the need for comprehensive reform in tax administration becomes necessary. In addition, tax reforms are tools used to eliminate tax evasion and tax avoidance practices in order to enhance tax revenue collections and remove tax distortions. Tax reforms involve restructuring the tax systems, tax administration, sub-systems and laws in order to enhance tax revenue collections. It also involves the introduction of measures that help to broaden the tax base while simultaneously flattening the tax rates.

Tax reforms are necessary for improvement of tax effectiveness not just avoiding tax evasion practices. The new tax reform paradigm looks at taxes primarily as the means to finance government expenditure (Azizul, 2001). Countries, which have experienced the challenges of tax collection due to narrow tax bases, can also embark on reforms in order to widen the tax base, increasing their tax nets such that they are able to include even some of the informal sector activities previously not included in the tax net.

6.2 OBJECTIVES OF TAX REFORMS

Despite the specific objectives, of undertaking tax reforms, a country may reform its tax laws in order to achieve the followings:

1. Remove or simplify complex tax laws- When the tax laws are complicated to understand and interpret, it makes tax collection and administration difficult to both for tax officials and taxpayers. The idea of reform will therefore to make the law simpler.
2. Enhance tax compliance – Tax law reform is necessary to ensure both voluntary and compulsory compliance. This at the end should help the government reduce the rate of tax evasion and avoidance in the country
3. Where the country has a narrow tax base, it cannot achieve its tax objectives. The reform becomes

necessary to widen the tax base and be able to collect more revenue.
4. Help to achieve efficient tax administration. The efficient tax administration will support government efforts in achieving high levels of tax compliance and tax collections.
5. Creation of semi-autonomous revenue authorities

6.3. GUIDING PRINCIPLES FOR TAX REFORMS

All tax reforms require guiding principles; otherwise, the results would not help a government in achieving its tax objectives. Odd and Rackner (2003) argue that a tax system of any country has to be judged on its ability to raise revenues, effect on economic efficiency, equity implications and administrative feasibility. The consideration of these principles is important from the time of planning the reforms to implementation of tax laws. Stein (1997) provides a number of guiding principles for tax reforms such as using lump sum taxes, focus on indirect taxes on final consumptions and need to ensure a trade- off between efficiency and equity on indirect taxation. The following principles are the common characteristics of tax reforms:

1. Simplicity- Any changes of tax laws should consider simplicity, which means that all laws must be simple to understand and comply by the taxpayer. Difficult tax laws force non- tax compliance and poor

administration. Simplicity means tax laws have to be written in a clear and concise language to both taxpayers and tax officials.

2. Transparency – Tax reforms have to be transparent, which means that tax rates should be known to taxpayers beforehand and should not be on secrecy basis. This also means that Taxpayers should know that a tax exists, how and when it is imposed upon them and others.
3. Minimizing non- tax compliance- Any reforms have to be guided by this principle which means that all changes in the tax systems and laws should not increase noncompliance which reduces government revenues.
4. Convenience – When it comes to payment, tax systems and laws should be convenient to both taxpayers and tax administration otherwise the government might not be able to collect enough taxes. Convenience also means that tax should be due at a time or in a manner that is most likely to be convenient for the taxpayer.
5. Promote of economic growth and efficiency- Tax reforms should not impair economic growth and efficiency of the economic sectors in the country but rather should create conducive environment for businesses and economic productive sectors to higher productivity which can lead to higher collection of taxes.
6. Cost-effective collection mechanism: The costs to collect a tax should be kept to a minimum for both

the government and taxpayers. If the government spends more money collecting tax revenue than amount collected then that system is not cost effective.
7. Positive impact on government revenue- Any tax reform should aim at helping the government to obtain positive impact on its revenue through tax laws and policies. The reforms on tax rates, structure, incentives, exemptions and other avenues should support government efforts in raising revenue and reducing deficit budgeting. In most cases, if the reforms adhere to this guiding principle, the government can be able to determine how much tax revenue is likely to be collected and when.

6.4. TREND OF TAX REFORMS IN DEVELOPING COUNTRIES

Most of the tax reforms that have taken place in African countries are a result of the recommended structural programs from the international financial institutions as a measure to redress tax under-collection problems. According to Odd & Rackner (2003), the common tax reforms in African countries included the abolition of export taxes, introduction of value added tax, lowering personal and corporate taxes. Other reforms include the simplification of the tax bands and broadening of the bases, reduction of import duties and simplification of the rate structure. These reforms are not so different from the ones which developed countries have carried over the past two decades.

Typical examples of tax reforms carried at East African countries in the last five years include the reduction of corporation tax to a uniform rate of 30% in Uganda and Tanzania and 37.5% in Kenya, which aimed at promoting investment in the region. In addition, an increase of the PAYE threshold which has promoted fairness to small tax payers, the introduction of VAT ranging from 16% – 18%, reasonable threshold for compulsory registration and tax base have been widened such as introduction of tax on rental income.

6.5. AVENUE FOR TAX REFORMS

Identification of tax reform areas of any country that wants to reform its tax system and laws are important. Proper studying of the tax laws in order to identify possible areas of loopholes and scanning the tax environment are key issues that can help to come up with good avenues for more tax collection. The proper avenues for more tax collection may vary from one tax jurisdiction to another.

However, the following are common areas, which most countries take into consideration when making the reforms

1. Reforming the income and corporate taxes- Countries that have reformed their income taxes and corporate taxes have reviewed their PAYE structure and have also changed how taxes are collected by ensuring that the payments of taxes are made through banks
2. Use of ICT Systems for Tax operations that have necessitated revenue to use e-filing of returns, Use of ASYCUDA, computerized motor vehicle registration and computerized driver license systems (Kitlya, 2011)
3. Reforming the tax administration
4. Widening the tax base to include possible tax net in the informal sector

6.6. CHALLENGES TO TAX REFORMS

Despite the efforts and strategies that countries will apply to reform their tax laws, a number of issues still pose challenges that countries face as they try to obtain maximum benefits from tax reforms. Lise & Gloppen (2002) argue that lack of tax culture in a country, the existence of large informal sector and lack of transparency and autonomy on tax reforms pose challenges to tax reform efforts. In trying to reform the tax administration countries experience challenges due to lack of capacities for implementing the tax administration, a weak regulatory framework that encourages cohesions and extra-legal tax enforcement. Bird (1983) argues about a challenge of introducing tax laws without cautions, which means that tax laws need not be introduced without carefully studying as it may lead to unnecessary changes of the tax laws within a short period of time which might have negative effects on tax collections.

PRACTICE QUESTIONS

Question 1

Discuss in details why countries might decide to reform its tax system and laws.

Question 2

What major tax reforms have been undertaken by your country in the past decade?

Question 3

What reforms do you think your country still need to make in order to achieve tax evasion and minimize tax evasion?

Question 4

What are the main characteristics of a tax system that can necessitate a country to undertake reforms?

Question 5

Which issues will necessitate a country to reform its tax administration system?

Question 6

What are the key ingredients of tax administration reforms?

Question 7

Select a country of your own and evaluate the tax reforms that were carried out in the past 5 years. Do the reforms facilitate tax compliance and fairness to the taxpayer?

Question 8

What are the implications on tax reforms in line with regional integrations?

Question 9

Discuss the pros and cons of tax reforms.

7. TAX INCENTIVES

❑ **Topic Objectives**
The topic will introduce to students the concept of Tax incentives and major objectives expected from these incentives

❑ **Coverage**
7.1 Introductions
7.2 Why tax incentives
7.3 Forms of Tax Incentives
7.4 Abuses of tax Incentives
7.5 Tax Incentives in Selected African countries
7.6 Similarities and Differences in Tax Incentives
Practice Questions

❑ **Learning Outcome**
At the end of the topic the reader should be able to appreciate why tax incentives are necessary for investment development in a country

CHAPTER 7

Tax Incentives

7.1 INTRODUCTION

Today Countries are faced with the dilemma of raising public revenue to fund public expenditures. Revenue can only be raised through tax and high taxes scare away investors who seek maximum returns on their investments. This challenge of raising revenue has been met by countries relying more heavily on indirect taxes than direct taxes. However, present days pose more challenges to countries to attract sustainable investments due to the fact that the global economy is more competitive such that less competitive countries might miss the opportunity to attract investors. In such competitive environment, Vera and Harvey (2000) argue that tax instruments such as the use of tax incentive can help in stimulating local and foreign investment which in turn create more investments; create jobs and other social and economic benefits. As a tax policy instrument, most developing countries have continued to use this as a strategy that gives a wide variety of special preferences to encourage investment broadly or in specific sectors and regions

According to UNCTAD (2000), tax incentives can be described as any incentive given by the government to local or foreigner investor that reduces or eliminates the tax burden in order to induce them to invest in particular projects or sectors. Tax incentives operate beyond the tax laws. Tax incentives objectives seek to give permission to deviate from the existing tax laws legally though more specific for specific companies and projects.

7.2. WHY TAX INCENTIVES

There are number of reasons and arguments as to why tax incentives should be given. Despite of the misuse and abuse of tax incentives in some countries, these tax incentives remain a major tool for attracting foreign investments. Kasaro and Kiria (2009) argue that tax incentives may be useful in some cases, such as to promote sensitive investments which at the end can address market failure and equity concerns.

Another argument for tax incentive in a country is to raise government tax revenues contribution to GDP. However, there are negative impacts of tax incentives to government revenue. Studies by various scholars from different countries including the one by Levin (2004) in Tanzania show that there is evidence that one of the factors that contribute to low tax revenue /GDP ratio is substantial tax incentives granted to new and ongoing investments.

7.3. FORMS OF TAX INCENTIVES

The type of tax incentives will differ from one country to another country depending on each country objectives. Different types of incentives can be availed by the government to meet specific objectives. Some of these incentives can work in some countries but fail in other countries. This depends on the country specific factors such as the level of economy and country specific tax objectives.

a. Tax Holiday
b. Tax Exemptions
c. Rebates
d. Government subsidies
e. Exemptions on Import duty
f. Exemptions on VAT

7.4. ABUSE OF TAX INCENTIVES

While tax incentives are expected to raise government revenue collections, unfortunately tax incentives have been reported to be abused in various countries across the globe through tax evasion, corruption and other schemes used by both local and foreign investors. In order to ensure minimal abuse of tax incentives, the government in a given country has to design proper mechanism that will help to minimize the abuse of tax incentives, otherwise the government will be losing huge amount of tax revenues.

There should be Mechanisms that can help to avoid or eliminate corruptions by tax officials who are likely to collude with investors to abuse the incentives. Collective decision making of giving tax exemption can be a good strategy to minimize tax incentives abuse. The abuse of tax incentives on the other side can demotivate other taxpayers who are not given the incentives, as it can demoralize to comply to tax laws when others are abusing the incentives.

7.5. TAX INCENTIVES IN SELECTED AFRICAN COUNTRIES

Tax incentives vary from one country to another. However, the objectives of tax incentives are not so different from the ones discussed above. For purpose of understanding tax incentives, few countries are selected to show how tax incentives are applicable.

7.5.1 NAMIBIA

The government of Namibia has special tax incentive package for stimulating economic growth and creation of employment. The package comprises of the following tax incentives:

I. GENERAL TAX INCENTIVES

These include the following incentives

- Nonresident shareholders tax is only 10 percent
- Dividends accruing to Namibian companies or resident shareholders are tax exempt
- Plant, Machinery and equipment can be fully written off over a period of three years
- Non –manufacturing operations can be written off, 20 percent in the first year and the balance at 4% over the ensuing 20 years.
- Import or purchase of manufacturing machinery and equipment is exempted from Value Added Tax (VAT)
- Preferential market access to USA and other markets for manufacturers and exporters is provided.

II. TAX INCENTIVES FOR MANUFACTURERS

Tax incentives for manufacturers include the following

1. Tax abatement- The government of Namibia allows 50% special tax deductions on the taxable income from manufacturing enterprises for a period of five years, to be phased out on the straight-line basis over a subsequent period of 10 years. The abatement is applicable to all operations approved and registered as manufacturers by the ministry of finance in consultation with the ministry of trade and industry.

2. Tax package for new investments- Where companies wish to establish a new manufacturing venture in Namibia or relocate an existing operation to Namibia, a special tax package may be negotiated through the ministry of trade and industry, which then makes recommendations to the Ministry of Finance. The Minister of Finance is empowered to grant, in consultation with the Minister of any line Ministry, special conditions to certain manufacturing enterprises on the rate of tax payable and the terms under which the rate shall apply.
3. Special Building Allowance- Buildings erected for manufacturing enterprises or manufacturing purposes (i.e. not including office buildings) can be written off at the rate of 20% in the first year and the balance at 8% per year over the ensuing 10 years.

III. TAX INCENTIVES FOR EXPORT PROMOTION ACTIVITIES

1. Non-tax incentives for manufacturers- This includes grants and loans for exporters to assist exporters in securing new markets, and exemption on costs incurred for industrial studies.
2. Incentives for exporters of manufactured goods- This includes the following the provision of Tax allowance on income derived from the export of manufactured goods. Taxable income derived from the export of manufacture goods with exception of

fish and meat products, whether they have been produced in Namibia or not shall be reduced by an allowance equal to 80 percent of the amount

3. Export processing Zone (EPZ) incentives on all enterprises which undertake manufacturing, assembly, re-packaging and break-bulk operations and gear all or almost all their production for exports. This makes such enterprises eligible for EPZ whereby they do not pay corporate tax, import tax and sales tax.

7.5.2 TANZANIA

Tax reform has been an important component of Tanzania's reform programme. In the 1980s and the early 1990s the reform aimed at simplifying the tax system and enhancing tax revenue collection.

Special attention in granting tax incentives are directed to lead and priority sectors such as agriculture, agro-based industries, mining, economic infrastructure, tourism, petroleum and gas sector. Priority Sectors: manufacturing, natural resources such as fishing and forestry, aviation, commercial building, financial services, transport, broadcasting, human resource development and export-oriented projects. Investors in these sectors enjoy zero import duty rates for importation of capital goods and deferment of VAT thereon. All incentives have a fiscal base, and are delivered through a reduction in, or exclusion from, tax or duty payments to investors in lead and priority sectors with investment above $300,000 in the case of foreign investors and above $100,000 in the case of local investors.

EXAMPLES OF TAX INCENTIVES IN TANZANIA

1. EPZ ACT 2006 AMENDED SECTION 21

- Exemption from value added tax on utility and wharf age charges
- Remission of customs duty, value added tax and any other tax payable in respect to importation of one administrative vehicle, ambulances, firefighting equipment vehicles and up to two buses for employees' transportation to and from the Export Processing Zones
- Exemption from payment of all taxes and levies imposed by the local government authorities for products produced in the Export Processing Zones for a period of ten years
- Exemption from payment of withholding tax on rent, dividends and interest for the first ten years;
- Exemption from payment of corporate tax for an initial period of ten years and thereafter a corporate tax shall be charged at the rate specified in the Income Tax Act, 2004
- Emission of custom duties, value added tax and any other tax charged on raw materials and goods of capital nature related to the production in the export processing zones

2. EAST AFRICA CUSTOMS MANAGEMENT ACT

- Non-taxation of imports of capital goods and raw materials
  Section 117(1) of EACMA Subject to the provisions of the Customs laws, goods imported in accordance with this section for a temporary use or purpose only shall be exempt from liability to import duties.

3. INCENTIVES UNDER VAT ACT 2006

Exportation of goods and services from the United Republic, supply by a local manufacturer of tractors for agricultural use, planters, harrows, combine harvesters, fertilizer distributors, liquid or powder sprayers for agriculture, spades, the supply by a local manufacturer of fertilizers, pesticides, insecticides, fungicides, herbicides are zero rated. Petroleum products, Tourist services are exempted for VAT purpose and Importation by or supply to a registered licensed drilling, mining, exploration or prospecting company of equipment to be used solely for drilling, mining, exploration or prospecting activities, the importation by or supply of capital goods to any person are granted special relief.

4. INCENTIVES UNDER INCOME TAX ACT (ITA 2004)

Capital allowances on investment goods for income tax purposes allowance is granted to a person for each item of plant or machinery, that is used in manufacturing processes and fixed in a factory, used in fish farming; or Used for providing services to tourists and fixed in a hotel calculated as 50 percent of the net cost of the asset at the time it is added to the pool. Plant and machinery (including windmills, electric generators and distribution equipment) used in agriculture Depreciation rate is 100%

Withholding tax from investment returns for a resident person on dividend, interest, natural resource payment, rent or royalty which has a source in the United Republic is not subject to withholding tax. Other incentives include the incentives for petroleum exploration and development such as the non-import duties on all equipment brought in for petroleum exploration and full allowance for unrecovered exploration costs incurred under earlier PSAs by the company in all its contract areas once it has made a discovery in a subsequent PSA.

7.5.3 KENYA

The Kenyan Government in its tax legislation has the following tax incentives for all categories of investors.

CAPITAL EXPENDITURE DEDUCTIONS

The income tax Act (Cap 470) under the second schedule has given investors who invest in the country tax incentives in the form of capital allowances. These include;

a. **Investment Deductions**:
The current rate for this type of allowance ranges

from 100% to 150% depending on the location of the investment. This is granted to investors who construct industrial buildings and buy machinery for manufacturing purposes and install it in the industrial buildings. It has also been extended to investors in the tourism sector and the education sector as well.

b. **Industrial Building Allowance**:

This allowance is granted to owners of industrial building at the rate of 2.5%-10% for industrial buildings meant for manufacturing purposes, hotels and educational Institution buildings.

c. **Wear and Tear Allowances**

This allowance is granted to investors who incur capital expenditure on machinery to cater for the annual wearing out of machinery due to use. The current rates range from a high of 37.5% for heavy machinery to 12.5% for office furniture and other machinery.

d. **Mining Investment Allowances**

This is granted to investors who engage in mining activities or prospecting for minerals in the country. It is granted to investors who engage in mining or incur expenditure of any nature before mining commences. While the rate is fixed at 40% for the 1st year, investors have been given the leeway to negotiate for higher rates with the tax authorities based on the estimated life of their mines.

e. Tax Holidays

Investors have been granted tax holidays of up to ten years if they invest in the Export Processing Zones (EPZ) or manufacture specifically for export. These investors do not pay any tax on their income for the 1st ten years of operation.

f. Lower Tax Rates

Any investor who manufactures for export within the export processing zones enjoys lower tax rates as compared to investors in other areas. With a tax a rate of 25% on the profits after the tax Holidays of 10 years, these investors pay a lower tax for the next 10 years.

g. Duty Remission

Those investors who invest in the country and import the following items pay no duty on the items. These include all raw materials imported for manufacturing processes, all machinery imported whether old or new and machinery imported for use in government funded projects.

h. Zero- rating for Value Added Tax (VAT) Purposes

Investors who manufacture for export purposes are eligible to claim any input tax deductions they pay on their inputs and charge VAT on all their export supplies at the rate of zero. This has the advantage of providing the investors with the motivation to set up industries in Kenya and enjoy the tax advantage of lower input costs as the tax they pay on their inputs is refunded by the government.

7.6. SIMILARITIES AND DIFFERENCES IN TAX INCENTIVES

By looking at the above discussion on tax incentives of the selected countries, we can easily note that there are similarities in many areas and sectors in terms of types of incentives that are available in each country such as tax holiday and exemptions. However, the differences are easily seen in the rates applicable in each incentive. The objectives of the incentives are also the same with varying degree of tones. From government point of view, tax incentives are aimed at promoting investment and increasing the tax contribution to the GDP and promoting local investment productive capacity.

It should also be noted that these incentives have not given the same results to all countries even the ones which have adopted similar incentives at the same time. Tax incentives have worked very well in some countries but not in other countries. A country like Rwanda, which adopted tax incentives similar to ones used by Uganda, has helped the country to attract more foreign investors than Uganda itself. This shows that the mechanism to operationalize these incentives is important, country specific factors and environment can also make the tax incentives more effective in attracting foreign investment.

PRACTICE QUESTIONS

Question 1

What are the main objectives of tax incentives?

Question 2

Select a country of your own choice. Study the tax incentives that are available. Evaluate the weaknesses of the available incentives and discuss how they can be improved in order to support the growth of both local and foreign investments.

Question 3

Briefly explain the types of incentives that are available in your country? Do the incentives support the growth of local investment?

Question 4

What types of incentives do you think can be used by the government to support growth of both local and foreign investments?

Question 5

What are the perquisite conditions that can make the investment effective?

8. INVESTMENT CLIMATE

❑ **Topic Objective**
To show to students the relationship between investments and taxation as well as show how the taxes affects the level of investments in their country.

❑ **Coverage**
8.1. Introduction
8.2 Africa Investment Climate
8.3. Challenges impairing the investment climate in Africa
8.4. The role of Governments in promoting investment climate
8.5. The Role of development partner's in promoting investments in Africa
8.6. Investment Climate in Selected Sub-Saharan Countries
Practice Questions

❑ **Learning Outcome**
At the end of the topic, students should be able to understand the investment climate operating in their own countries and advice their government on how to improve it.

CHAPTER 8

Investment Climate

8.1. INTRODUCTION

The investment climate is an environment that facilitates both local and foreign investments. The existence of proper legal mechanisms in a country, stable political environment, supportive monetary and fiscal policies as well as availability of proper infrastructure, natural resources, skilled and unskilled workers is an indicator or a sign of good investment climate. These factors are critical success factors for viable investments. Investment climate comprises the political, economic, social and technological environment. Political environment encompasses the stability of a government that can assure investors on the predictability of their future survival. It is an environment where there is security and non- political interference. The economic environment is broader as it includes such issues as the level of economic infrastructures, availability of markets and economic policies that support investment growth.

The social environment includes the labor relations.

For example, where there is no minimum wage already set by the government it can be good for the investor in the short run, but in the long run workers are affected and the employer/employee relationship can be broken down, which then lowers employees' work productivity. The technology environment is the one, which supports the existence of modern technology that supports both local and foreign investments. On the other hand, it should be able to promote local technology.

8.2 AFRICA INVESTMENT CLIMATE

The investment climate in Africa varies from one country to another, depending on a number of factors and other prevailing conditions. There is a belief that the investment climate in Africa is partly conducive while in other parts it is not conducive enough to attract investors. In times of political instability, the climate is not conducive for foreign investors. Consider the case of Zimbabwe, Uganda especially the northern part, Sudan, Ivory Coast and Somalia. These areas in the above-mentioned countries do not provide a good environment for foreign investment. They are characterized by political instability, lack of proper institutions, lack of proper investment policies, human rights violation and no political will support for investments as well as poor infrastructure.

As already mentioned above, the investment climate in some of the African countries is open for investment in many areas. The availability of un- tapped natural resources makes those countries a potential area for many types of investments. Africa has potential land, mines, forestry and many other resources, which are untapped potential for investments.

There are some countries in Africa, which have a good investment climate, environment such as Tanzania, Mauritius and South Africa, though there is no guarantee of permanent political stability. We also know that politics in Africa is difficult to predict. These countries, though they are not all at the same level, have adequate infrastructure, good and attractive investment policies, cheap labor and availability of untapped natural resources. At the same time, some of these countries have macroeconomic stability and an enabling environment for private sector activity and industrial growth.

These countries also have an independent judiciary system and effective regulatory framework. Investors are also free to repatriate capital investments as well as dividends, management fees, interests, profits and royalties. These countries protect investment and property rights, which are government guarantees through investment acts. These governments may do so by stipulating that expropriation of foreign investments has to involve payments in proper amount and full compensation at the market value. The Government should allow foreign investors to transfer the funds in the original currency of the investment.

These countries also belong to the Multilateral Investment Guarantee Agency (MIGA), United Nations Commission on International Law and they have signed other multilateral, regional and bilateral investment protection agreements. They have also signed a number of international agreements on patents and intellectual property, including those of the World Intellectual Property Organization (WIPO), Paris Union, African Regional Industrial Property Organization (ARIPO) and the Universal Copyright Convention of UNESCO.

8.3 IMPAIRMENT: AFRICA INVESTMENT CLIMATE

Despite of good avenues for investments as described above, there are many challenges that impair investment growth in African countries. African countries need to address these challenges.

1. RESTRICTIVE MOVEMENT OF FOREIGN EXCHANGE

Some countries restrict free movement of foreign exchange although most countries have now liberalized their monetary policies to allow for its free movement. An example of countries where so far there is restriction of foreign exchange is Ethiopia and Seychelles. The restriction of free movement of foreign exchange is a setback for prospective investors. No investor would be interested to invest in a country where there is no freedom to transfer funds to his or her home country. The restrictions by few countries which are remaining is due to their political backgrounds and other economic problems.

2. POLITICAL RISK

In some countries, there is a high political risk, which threatens foreign investors. The trend of nationalization of private property can still be possible in some countries, although most African countries have forsaken this culture. Some African countries still have civil wars, high level of political instability and frequent change of governments, which are not smooth and predictable. All of these have a great negative impact on the investment climate and reduce the level of an investor confidence.

3. HIGH LEVEL OF CORRUPTION

The level of corruption in some African countries is very high which creates many bureaucratic processes to investment growth. The corruption ranges from white corruption to petty corruption. A number of studies conducted in some African countries indicate a high level of corruption thus impairing investment growth in these countries.

4. DISPUTE SETTLEMENTS

Where there are disputes between an investor and the host government as far as investment is concerned, the courts in Africa are not effective due to corruption and slow process to solve the disputes.

5. UNDERDEVELOPED FINANCIAL AND CAPITAL MARKETS

The financial and capital market in Africa is underdeveloped. The impact of this is on the ability of the investors to raise funds in the local market. The market is still very shallow as compared to developed countries. Companies cannot raise funds very easily as there are few banks and few financial instruments. In other words, the firms are limited to extend their capital structure. Even where capital markets exist in some of these countries, listing requirements in the stock exchange are not supportive for many companies, which want to obtain listings.

6. INFRASTRUCTURE

Most countries in Africa experience major problems in their infrastructure, which is the key to development of investments. Poor roads or no roads at all, electricity problems, inadequate financial institutions, communication problems characterize most of these countries. Government of these countries undertakes number of efforts to improve their infrastructures despite of the funding limitations, already experienced.

7. SUBSISTENCE ECONOMIES

Most African countries have subsistence economies where the incomes of the citizen are very small such that the propensity to save is almost zero and the purchasing power is very low. Despite of the comparative advantage African countries have in terms of abundant natural resources these countries still depend on rain for their agriculture production and less modern technology to facilitate agriculture production.

8. LOW LEVEL OF TECHNOLOGY AND UNSKILLED WORKERS

Most African countries lack a high level of technology and a skilled workforce. Asian countries have attracted more foreign investments as they have a high level of technology and a high number of skilled workers simply because Multinational companies can easily deploy them in their productive industries as compared to Africa.

9. FOREIGN EXCHANGE RATE PROBLEMS

The existence of volatile exchange rates characterizes most African countries. Foreign exchange rates in Africa cannot be easily predictable due to the changing economic conditions. This is because of a number of factors such as the civil wars and political instability in some of these countries.

10. HIGH BORROWING INTEREST RATES

High borrowing interest rates impair the funding of businesses in African countries. Financial institutions charge very high rates of interest, thus impairing local companies in raising funds through debts.

11. GOVERNANCE FACTORS

There are a number of governance factors, which are critical for the success of investment in Africa. These include investment incentives, the effectiveness of the legal system, land and law administration as well as the speed of decision making in all institutions directly or indirectly linked to promotion of investments. Lagging behind on governance issues is likely to hinder the growth of investments.

12. FINANCIAL FACTORS

These are also critical for boosting investment opportunities. They include the level of inflation, availability of business finance, interest rates and exchange controls. These factors can work against the tide of investment growth in a country.

8.4. GOVERNMENTS ROLE IN PROMOTING INVESTMENT CLIMATE

The efforts already undertaken by African countries over the past years in promoting investment growth are worth mentioning here. Although there is still much more effort that is needed, these initiatives are likely to take investment in Africa to higher levels. These initiatives include the following;

1. Entering into a bilateral investment agreement with developed countries
2. Signing double taxation treaties with developed countries
3. Adoption of the COMESA common investment area agreement, which envisages a free investment area for member countries with the major intention of making the region an attractive destination for both regional and international investors
4. The Economic Community of West African States (ECOWAS) created a department responsible for promoting cross border investments and joint venture businesses in the region.

Despite these efforts, more efforts are important to improve a favorable investment climate in Africa to enable foreign investors to feel comfortable in shifting their investment from developing countries. Governments have a major role in creating the required environment. A good investment climate has attracted FDIs from developing countries largely, although African countries have not managed to attract more than the Asian countries in the last decade.

Governments in Africa can support the creation of good investment climate by doing the following:

1. Harmonizing the investment incentives and regimes in the region such as the removal of all tariff barriers
2. Remove the restriction on investments by foreign investors in some economic sectors, such as

power generation sector and ports. Many African countries restrict investments in power generation in the public sectors.
3. African countries should also be concerned with the development of economic infrastructure that hinders trade facilitations.
4. African countries should give high priority to yon local capacity building investments. African countries need to invest in technological advancement that can contribute to the enhancement of various economic sectors.
5. Non-membership to international organizations that deal with resolutions of disputes as far as investments conflicts are concerned is a discouragement to foreign investors. African countries should join such international organizations and adhere to clauses that require them to compensate foreign investors in case of property expropriations. This move will motivate and attract foreign investors.
6. African countries' financial and capital markets are still very shallow as compared to developed countries. Therefore, t African countries should put more emphasis on developing their financial and capital markets.

8.5. DEVELOPMENT PARTNERS AND INVESTMENT PROMOTION IN AFRICA

Over the past decade, we have seen a number of development partners from developed countries that have developed interest and supported the promotion of investments in Africa. Examples of these partners are countries like China, Japan, United States of America and some international organizations like the Commonwealth Secretariat, European Free Trade Area (EFTA) and the Organization for Economic Cooperation and Development (OECD). The development initiatives of these countries and organization aim at promotion of private and international investment in Africa, Protection of intellectual property and Promoting the review and modernization of trade related investments legislation with aim of harmonizing it to the trade commitments.

8.6. INVESTMENT CLIMATE: SELECTED SUB –SAHARAN AFRICAN COUNTRIES

It is good to have an overview of investment climate of few countries in selected few developing countries especially the less developed countries. The following few countries in East and Southern African countries are representative of majority countries in these two regional blocks;

8.6.1. UGANDA

The investment climate in Uganda is conducive for attracting foreign investments. It was not possible to attract foreign investment during the past two decades, as there was too much violent, internal strife, which led to civil wars. Now, Uganda has attracted foreign investors from the Middle East and Asia. The ability to attract foreign investment shows that the investment climate is good and this is a contribution of the following factors;

a. The country is open to foreign investment by providing attractive incentives for medium and long-term investors. The Heritage Foundation's 2009 economic index listed Uganda's economy at number 63 out of 165 countries, and as the fourth freest economy of 46 countries in Sub-Saharan Africa, based on factors such as the ease of doing business, openness to trade, property rights, fiscal and monetary policy.
b. The country has policies, laws and regulations that are favorable towards foreign investors. The government has done many reforms on its monetary and fiscal policies to attract foreign investments.
c. There is improved infrastructure such as good roads, airports and improved communication services. The Government of Uganda has spent a lot of money to ensure that there are good roads, sewage systems, electricity generation that will support economic development in the country

d. Uganda keeps open capital accounts, and the Ugandan law imposes no restrictions on capital transfers in and out of Uganda. Investors can obtain foreign exchange and make transfers at commercial banks without approval from the Bank of Uganda (BOU, the Central Bank) in order to repatriate profits, dividends, and make payments for imports and services.

e. Uganda is a member of the Multilateral Investment Guaranty Agency (MIGA) and the International Centre for the Settlement of Investment Disputes (ICSID). By being members in these international organizations, foreign investors have confidence of investing in the country. At the same time the country's constitution, guarantees prompt payment of fair and adequate compensation, prior to the taking over of possession or acquisition of the property. All these increase the confidence of investors. The constitution guarantees any person who has an interest or right over expropriated property access to a court of law.

8.6.2. KENYA

Kenya is one of the countries in East Africa that has a good climate for investment despite other factors, which act as negative incentives to foreign investors. During the period of 1960's and 1970's the country, was the prime choice by many foreign investors. Since the 1980's, however, the country has experienced a drop in the number of foreign investors as the result of rising corruption, poor governance and deterioration of infrastructures.

In order to make the country more attractive for foreign investment, the government of Kenya undertook a number of reforms on its investment policy, monetary and fiscal policies. To date there are more than 200 Multinational Corporations in Kenya investing in various economic sectors. These reforms included among others;

   a. Introduction of market- based reforms, which has provided more incentives for both local and foreign private investment. Foreign investors seeking to establish a presence in Kenya generally receive the same treatment as local investors, but there are some exceptions.
   b. Streamlining the administrative and legal procedures to achieve a more effective investment climate
   c. Setting of the minimum foreign investment threshold at $500,000
   d. Harmonizing the investment regimes and incentives among the original East African Community (EAC) countries (Tanzania, Kenya and Uganda)
   e. Improving infrastructure that can facilitate investment growth in the country

8.7.3. TANZANIA

Tanzania is a highly ranked country in Africa as far as peace and political stability is concerned. Despite of its multiparty democracy system, it is the most peaceful country as it is the center of economic and political stability in the sub-Sahara African region. This reduces the political risks to investors and gives them confidence.

Other characteristics of Tanzania, which make the country's investment climate conducive, are the availability of skilled Labour resulting from the efforts of the government to develop and train its people. Very few professions are now lacking in the country since it has improved its human capabilities and encouraged technology transfer as a pre-condition for enhancing investment growth.

Over the past decade Tanzania has improved the level of its infrastructures by building good quality roads, improved its airports and ports in order to facilitate the transportation sector. Tanzania is one of those countries, which have many untapped natural resources such as minerals, big land, as well as abundance of wildlife attractions. All these make it a favorable destination for investment of any kind.

Tanzania has a very good regulatory framework for investment. Over years, the country has been reforming its regulatory framework for business licensing and investment in order to allow foreign investors to register their businesses and investments with minimal bureaucratic procedures. The establishment of Tanzania Investment Centre and the Investment Code are the key indicators that the country's investment climate is becoming friendlier to prospective investors.

The reform of investment incentives and guarantees

is another positive feature of good investment climate in Tanzania. Tanzania offers various fiscal incentives to foreign investors such as tax holidays in the first five years of investment and exemption of VAT for imported capital goods. In order to attract foreign investors, the country has also signed a number of double taxation treaties with various countries. It has also signed a number of multilateral and bilateral agreements on protection and promotion of foreign investments.

8.7.5. ZIMBABWE

The emphasis of the government has been on the indigenization policy with a very defensive approach towards foreign investments. This policy, which requires foreign investments to have joint venture with locals at least with 30% participation, has remained strong in the country. However, the effect of this policy in the end is not yet clear.

8.7.6. RWANDA

Rwanda is one of those countries in the East African region whose economy is growing very fast despite of the genocide that occurred in 1994. Rwanda has created the Rwanda Development Board, which has reduced bureaucracy in investment. Now, business investors take only a day to register business in Rwanda if they follow all rules and regulations.

All sectors authorized to provide services to macro and micro businesses are brought under a single umbrella to avoid unnecessary harassment of the clients. This has improved the economic status and elimination of the bureaucracy, which has speeded business activities. If the current trend in Rwanda continues, this country is likely to be a developed country soon.

PRACTICE QUESTIONS

Question 1

It is believed that African Countries have poor investment Climate. Do you agree?

Question 2

Discuss whether African countries still need further reforms in their fiscal policies to attract more foreign investors.

Question 3

Evaluate the investment Climate of African Countries What are the main problems experienced and what can be done to alleviate the problems?

Question 4

What types of tax incentives are available in your country that support the growth of investments in your country?

9. TAX COMPLIANCE

❏ Topic Objective
The topic will introduce the students to the concept of tax compliance

❏ Coverage
9.1. Introduction
9.2. Pillars of Tax Compliance
9.3. Causes of non- tax compliance
9.4. Level of Tax Compliance
9.5. Strategies for Tax Compliance
Practice Questions

❏ Learning Outcomes
At the end of the topic, students should be able to understand the causes of non- tax compliance in their countries and know how to enhance tax compliance for their governments

CHAPTER 9

Tax Compliance

9.1 INTRODUCTION

Tax compliance is a key cornerstone for a country's achievement of its tax objectives. Tax compliance is the degree to which extent taxpayers comply or fails to comply with the tax rules of his country Jackson and Milton (1986) has defined tax compliance as the reporting of tax liability to the relevant authority in compliance with the applicable tax laws. In View of Palil and Mustapha (2011) tax compliance is the process by which taxpayers file all the required tax returns by declaring all income accurately and paying the exact tax liability using applicable tax laws and regulations. Non-tax compliance reduces government revenues, hence a setback for meeting its public expenditure, which can lead to deficit balance of payments. Tax compliance can be voluntary or by force of the relevant tax authority in a given jurisdiction (Van Dijke and Vrbroom, 2010). The responsibility of tax administration in any country is to foster voluntary tax compliance by using all possible methods including penalties. However, uses of penalties make tax compliance a compulsory issue and not voluntary action by taxpayers.

Tax compliance is broad in the sense that the areas of compliance that the taxpayer is required to comply are many. The compliance is required at registration stage where all tax systems require the registration of all taxpayers. The tax system also requires taxpayers to file and lodge their returns and keep proper books of accounts for their business affairs. Compliance also requires taxpayers to pay their tax obligations on the tax amount at required time immediately.

Therefore, we can say that compliance to tax laws by the taxpayers requires compliance on all of the mentioned areas although the level of compliance may vary in degree depending on the understanding or ignorance of tax laws by the taxpayer and intentional fraud by the taxpayers.

9.2 THE PILLARS OF TAX COMPLIANCE

In order for a country to succeed in achieving high level of tax compliance whether voluntarily or compulsory, the following measures have been necessary to promote the principle of compliance. These following measures are the main pillars to tax compliance;

A: PUBLIC RELATIONS

Proper public relationship between taxpayers and tax administration will enhance tax compliance. The purpose of such relationship is to build up appropriate tax environment in order to enhance tax compliance, improve mutual understanding and trust between taxpayers and tax authorities and enhance public knowledge of taxation. Most countries' tax authorities have special departments to deal with public relations for the aim of enhancing tax compliance.

B: TAX EDUCATION

Tax education to taxpayers is part of public relation that can help to create awareness. The complexity of tax laws and multiplicity of the tax laws makes compliance by the taxpayers difficult; unless taxpayers are educated then they can easily comply. The target audience for tax education should comprise the existing taxpayers and future potential taxpayers such as students.

Tax education can involve various strategies such as the use of media (example the use of special education programmes through Television programmes). The distribution of printed tax education materials to taxpayers such as brochures and conducting taxpayer's workshop can enhance the knowledge of taxpayer's compliance.

It is very important that Education programmes are designed in such a way that they can help taxpayers to understand the importance of paying taxes, help taxpayers to understand the existing tax laws and their tax obligations, whether they do business as sole proprietors, partnerships, or companies and give clear understanding of the tax laws that are difficult for interpretation by common individuals.

C: TAX CONSULTATION AND COUNSELING

The objective of tax counselling is to assist taxpayers in matters related to tax and to encourage voluntary submission of accurate tax returns and payment of taxes. Tax counselling becomes more effective where there are qualified, competent and committed staffs in the tax revenue department who are capable of providing advice on the interpretation of tax laws and procedures for filing tax returns.

D: GUIDANCE

Tax administration has a responsibility of providing individuals and groups with necessary guidance on how to improve business records keeping and tax returns. This can enhance taxpayer's compliance so that they can voluntarily file tax returns and pay taxes appropriately.

E. AUDITING AND EXAMINATION

One key pillar of tax compliance is auditing and examination, as a responsibility of tax authorities. This involves the capability of the tax officials to detect fraud, evasion and non-compliance. The possibility of auditing and examination creating the fear of being caught is high so that could be sufficient to act a deterrent. Auditing and examination is easily facilitated where the tax officials are well trained and have good working conditions.

It is important that tax officials have to obtain adequate training and better understanding of tax laws and have capacity of interpreting the existing tax laws as well as obtain exposure to international tax issues. Educated and experienced tax officials are likely to formulate successfully tax compliance strategies.

F. PENALTY PROVISIONS

Most countries tax laws provide for penalties for non-tax compliance. Existing of penalty provision is not necessarily that taxpayers will comply with tax laws if the tax authorities do not undertake criminal prosecution to violations of laws in respect of cases involving fraud or evasion. In some cases, publishing of names of tax evaders can help as a deterrent.

9.3 CAUSES OF NON-TAX COMPLIANCE

There are various causes of non-tax compliances. The factors we mention below are the common ones, which you can find in most of countries.

a. Taxpayers altitude is affected by her/his satisfaction or lack of satisfaction with her terms of trade with the government (Richupan 1987). When taxpayers are not happy with how tax revenue are utilized by the government they tend to be discouraged in paying taxes, hence opt to avoid or evade. Alim et al (1992) study suggest that compliance increases with the availability of public goods and services

b. When there is high rate of corruption by tax officials and bad examples set out by senior public and political leaders. This concurs with Snavely (1990) arguments that compliance tax behavior of the individual may be affected by the behavior of an individual reference group such as relatives, leaders, neighbors and friends

c. Lack of taxpaying culture. In African countries taxpaying culture is low as majority taxpayers are not aware of the importance of paying taxes, discouraged by the fact that there is no relationship between tax paid by the taxpayers and public services provided by the government.
d. When there are high taxes rates levied by the government then taxpayers are likely to indulge themselves in tax evasion or avoidance activities
e. Obsolete tax/ outdated tax laws give room for avoidance of taxes
f. Poor public relations between the revenue department/authority and the taxpayers
g. Poor response to tax education programmes by the public
h. Where the coverage area by the revenue department or revenue authority is small, then reaching some of potential taxpayers becomes difficult and impossible.
i. Higher illiteracy level is a hindrance to tax compliance
j. Complex tax laws which are difficult to understand and interpret by both taxpayers and tax officials
k. Inadequate tax education across the whole country
l. corruption
m. Complex legislation
n. Low levels of tax knowledge

o. Government non- accountability
p. Poor tax paying culture
q. Weak tax administration.
r. weak economies

9.4 LEVELS OF TAX COMPLIANCE

It is important for governments to measure the level of tax compliance in order to know to what extent tax objectives are achieved. The level of tax compliance can be high or low and can be supportive in achieving the desired objectives of taxation. Low level indicates non-supportive and it is likely to impair country economic development. There are number of issues, which we can look at them that can help to show the extent to which tax compliance level is supportive to tax objectives. The level of compliance is not supportive to achievement of tax objectives if the following issues frequently feature in the country

1. When there is low level of filling tax returns and even those who file their return they under-report their incomes.
2. When there is low tax GDP ratio, which means the percentage of contribution of tax to country GDP is very low.
3. Persistent deficit balance of payment to the government. This can lead to inability of the government to finance its budget rather depend more on donor funds. When this is a situation, the

government is unable to pay adequately and timely salaries.

9.5 STRATEGIES FOR ENHANCING TAX COMPLIANCE

Strategies to enhance tax compliance will differ from one country to another. However, the following strategies are common in majority east African and Sub-Saharan African countries

1. Creation of the revenue authority as a separate entity from the ministry of finance. In some countries such as Namibia and Swaziland, tax administration is still under the ministry of finance, which on one way it is a setback for tax compliance.
2. Existence of penalties or imprisonment for non-tax compliers.
3. Countries having or undergoing continuous tax reforms. This can help to discover loopholes in the tax laws that need a reform for high compliance.
4. Existence of systems that imparts tax payer education through the client care departments, exhibitions in -trade fairs and agriculture show events.
5. Audit and investigations coverage and intensity increased
6. Use of the Whistle blower system
7. Recognition of taxpayers on tax payer's days with trophies being won

8. Use of the media to educate tax payers of their obligations and rights
9. Use of Websites on the internet to provide information to taxpayers
10. Use of electronic fiscal devices that are given to taxpayers free of charge
11. Staff development programmes to enhance tax collection capacities
12. Taxpayer/client education
13. Intensified investigations and audits by tax authorities
14. Penalization of those found on the wrong side of the law and prosecution.
15. Awards to whistleblowers
16. Recognition of compliant taxpayers/clients

9.6 TAX COMPLIANCE LESSONS

Most countries that have successfully achievement in tax compliance have developed different strategies, which in the end have helped in increasing the tax revenues. In review of various literature and survey these strategies have been in use in various developed countries and other countries can adopt them to tax laws

1. Use of Integrated information management system. (South Africa, United Kingdom) where there is there is a high level of automation of the tax system. This can easily enable tax authorities to detect non-compliance easily.

2. Accountability and appropriate utilisation of taxes in the developed countries-this makes people more compliant
3. E-filing –cost of compliance is lowered- Developed countries no longer use manual system rather adopted e-filling where taxpayers are able to file their returns online. Example of such countries include South Africa, Canada, Singapore and United Kingdom
4. E-banking/payment
5. Provide specialised training for auditors and investigators
6. Have a tax management system that is comprehensive
7. Enhance exchange programs between authorities
8. Linking databases of various government departments
9. Offering amnesties to non-compliant clients for some time
10. Offer payment plan arrangements
11. Have a tax management system which has all the information about the registered clients' transactions
12. Provision of specialized training in for auditors and investigators
13. Customer service efforts
14. Increase revenues by enforcing compliance
15. Exchange programs between Revenue Authorities
16. Linking various databases like deeds databases, company registration databases

17. Provide assistance to compliant taxpayers
18. Measures to encourage taxpayers with untaxed overseas assets to step forward and declare their offshore wealth and avoid criminal prosecution by paying up the taxes they owe.
19. Improved tax administration through continuous training & systems improvement.
20. Review of Regulatory framework.

PRACTICE QUESTIONS

Question 1

Discuss the main causes of non-tax compliance in your country.

Question 2

What strategies are available in your country that can help in reducing the level of non-tax compliance?

Questions 3

Discuss how the government in your country can strengthen the pillars of tax compliance.

Question 4

What is the role of tax education in enhancing the level of tax compliance?

10. TAX HARMONIZATION

❑ Topic Objective
The topic will introduce the students to the concept of tax harmonization and its role in regional integrations

❑ Coverage
10.1 Introduction
10.2 Objectives of Tax Harmonization
10.3. What entails tax Harmonization
10.4 Regional Integration
10.5. Benefits of Tax harmonization in regional integration
10.6 Area of Tax Harmonization
10.7. Prerequisite issues for complete tax harmonization
Practice Questions

❑ Learning Outcomes
At the end of the topic students will be able to understand the reasons as to why tax harmonization is important in regional integrations.

CHAPTER 10

Tax Harmonization

10.1 INTRODUCTION

The concept of tax harmonization is not a new concept. Tax harmonization involves the use of same tax laws among different tax jurisdictions. Over time tax harmonization was applicable in Africa during the era of colonialism where two or more countries that were under the same rule of colonial master used same tax laws. Consider the case of Tanzania, Kenya and Uganda during the era of the British colony period, all countries used the same tax laws. This means that individual countries had no tax sovereignty as all tax laws, regulations and procedures were determined by British Government. Following independences of majority African Countries, countries were able to enact their tax laws though they were more inclined to follow the tax laws of their colonial masters. Tax Harmonization has gained momentum following regional integrations such as the one with European union countries and East Africa Community Integration (EAC).

Successfully implantation of tax harmonization might

involve a variety of steps. Cano (1996) elaborated various steps that are involved in tax harmonization which include standardization, comparability and cooperation. Standardization means having the same tax laws, equalizing tax burdens imposed on the same item under equal circumstances such as the use of same Common tariffs in EAST Africa Integration. Comparability does not necessarily mean the same thing as standardization but it involves the adjusting of tax structure to counteract the distortion of tax differences in regional integration.

It also involves the harmonization of tax regulations, tax bases and harmonization of institutions in terms of tax administration and follow-up mechanisms. Cooperation entails existence of reciprocal mutual assistance between tax jurisdiction, creating bilateral and multilateral cooperation mechanism, use of homogenous tax administration as well as the adoption of same tax laws interpretations. Cooperation may involve other necessary issues tax coordination.

10.2. WHAT IS INVOLVED IN TAX HARMONIZATION

The process of tax harmonization will involve the change of country tax laws in order to have tax laws similar to the ones with the countries in the regional blocks and having similar tax structure. This process has to be founded on the harmonization of the policies and procedures for tax administration in the respective regional block as well as the harmonization of specific tax rates. It is important that the process takes into account the priorities on specific policies that have impact the impact to the development economic activities and the businesses in respective countries in the regional blocks. The harmonization process has to be gradual to avoid any unnecessary negative impacts of the harmonization that have taken hurriedly without proper impact studies.

10.3. REGIONAL INTERGRATION

Regional integration is a process in which states enter into a regional agreement in order to enhance regional cooperation through regional institutions and rules Regional integrations brings a lot of benefits to all member countries though at different degree. However, the degree of the impact of the benefits of integration may vary from one country to another. The following are the benefits, which can be derived from regional integrations;

One of the benefit of Regional integration is to removes the trade barriers among member countries and facilitates movement of goods, services and people. Member countries enjoy doing trade without barriers as there are few or no restrictions. Trade tariffs and other restrictions that impair goods flow are also removed. The cost of doing business in region blocks normally comes down due to availability of expertise (World Bank, 2000)

It is also evidenced that Regional integration results into cost sharing on regional projects. Such projects could be regional infrastructure development projects such as the road and rail construction projects. An example are the joint regional efforts on projects which are aimed at fighting drug trafficking across number of African regional blocks which reduces individual member countries costs in doing the work alone.

According to Schiff and Winteres (2003) regional blocks have created common markets for member countries products. Member countries are free to trade among themselves thus having assured markets even before thinking of selling their products to developed countries. In integrations, market sizes increase with some clients moving closer to companies hence cutting down transport costs.

Regional integrations help member countries to coordinate their positions thus helping them to stand in multilateral negotiations with at least more visibility and possibly with stronger bargaining power. The integration can help countries to develop common positions and to bargain as a group rather than on a country by country basis, which would contribute to increased visibility, credibility and even better negotiation outcomes.

Regional integration brings about harmonization of monetary policies, fiscal policies, tax laws and standardization of products based on international principles. This again on other side it can help to reduce the prices of goods as the result of availability of goods and services.

10.4. CHALLENGES OF REGIONAL TAX HARMONIZATION

Tax harmonization is not always easy to achieve among different countries simply because different taxes and policies exist in among countries and it is difficult to find common ground. Since each country has a sovereign power to enact tax laws without being intervened by another country, it requires a common consensus to have common laws, which might not always easy.

The other challenges are that majority of countries would fear that tax integration will lead to erosion of fiscal autonomy and hence a need to avoid tax harmonization. At the same time Resistance from the private sector who fear opening up of competition may impair the process. The private sector plays a major role in the fiscal aspects of a country. Where the private sector is worried in facing external competitors it is likely that major obstacles for implementing tax harmonization will be resisted to avoid competition.

Where the Legal frameworks of the partner members states is not supportive, tax harmonization may be delayed which has the same impact posed by political set-up of member states.

Differences in Macro-economic conditions of the members states and level of economic development and level of Infrastructure, IT Development and institutional development plays a major role in enhancing harmonization process.

The other challenge pertains to harmonization is due to the fact that countries making up the regional blocks basically have different economic levels. This is due to the fact that some countries have broad tax base than others. And harmonization in this scenario has the potential of completely taking away much needed funds in some member countries in the block resulting in fear by individual members countries to accept putting their rates at par with the others.

On the other side, it is difficult for the countries in the regional blocks to have same tax rates due to the fact that each has its own development objectives that may not align with the common objective of the block.

It is considered that political reasons also matter much. A critical view of the member countries show that many are unable to harmonize taxes because each one of them tends to have a different political agenda. An exemplification of this is the reduction of tax rates in pre-election period for purposes of wooing voters for the ruling elite. The challenge here is that in most instances politicians tend to gratify personal desires first before the interests of the nation.

The third point is about sovereignty. On this aspect countries are afraid to lose their autonomy by giving in to conditions set in agreements signed at the regional block level. They do not in short want their national interests to be subordinate to regional blocks preferences.

Fourthly is the influence that historical background of a nation has on the policy towards tax and in addition to this is the attachments to other regional blocks whose agreements may not favor tax harmonization at the block level. This may better be captioned as reflecting conflicting preferential interests between the state parties.

10.5. AREAS OF TAX HARMONIZATION

Tax harmonization can involve various areas though effective gradual adoption is important. Despite of the steps of tax harmonization discussed above, there are areas where tax harmonization can be sought include

1. Harmonization of Income Taxes –This can include income tax and corporate taxes
2. Harmonization of VAT- Value added Taxes
3. Harmonization of Custom Tariffs
4. Harmonization of Excise duty
5. Harmonization of Investment incentives
6. Harmonization of rules, procedures and policies
7. Harmonization of Import tariff

It is important to note that the above-mentioned areas would be considered important because harmonization of taxes in them would entail the following: reduction in distortions in taxes, remove harmful tax competition, reduce administration and tax compliance costs and also reduce smuggling on high taxed goods.

10.6. PRELEQUISITE ISSUES PRIOR TO COMPLETE TAX HARMONIZATION

The challenges for reaching complete tax harmonization are many. Addressing these challenges pave a way for countries that want to enjoy the benefits of tax harmonization. The following are the main issues that countries that need to the regional integration need to address before reaching full tax harmonization.

1. Amendment of the country legal framework to harmonize it to the legal framework of other countries that are part of tax harmonization program
2. Tax harmonization process must be built on the principle of good corporate governance
3. Countries involved in the tax harmonization must align themselves on the state priorities, improved commitment and political will.
4. There should be deepened regional integrations across regional blocks

10.7. CONCLUSION

Though they are many challenges to the need for tax harmonization as seen in the foregoing discussion, it has also been demonstrated that they are some feasible areas that harmonization can be attained. In conclusion therefore, regional harmonization of taxes is not a far-fetched dream. It is something that can be done. Everything to change needs an agent and so we are beginning this day.

PRACTICE QUESTIONS

Question 1

Discuss the Challenges that impair tax harmonization in the regional integrations such as EAC and COMESA?

Question 2

What are the issues that need to be addressed before complete tax harmonization is reached in the regional integrations?

Question 3

What areas are good areas for tax harmonization in SADC/ EAC member countries and why do you think is important? Are there areas which you thing they are feasible for harmonization?

11. TAX INVESTIGATION

❑ **Topic Objective**
This topic is designed with the objective of introducing students to the concept of tax investigation.

❑ **Coverage**
11.1. Introduction to tax Investigations
11.2. Importance of tax investigations
11.3. Possible areas for tax investigations
11.4. Challenges of Tax Investigation
11.5. Streamlining tax investigation function
11.6. Tax investigation Framework
Practice Questions

❑ **Learning Outcome**
At the end students will appreciate why tax investigation is important for enhancing government revenue collection

CHAPTER 11

Tax Investigation

11.1. INTRODUCTION

Tax investigation is a process that follows a suspect on tax revenue under-reporting, tax evasion or tax avoidance by the taxpayers. Where the revenue authority discovers or suspect any practice that indicates any undercover of revenues, an in- depth investigation will be carried as an attempt to reveal the practice and recover revenues. Therefore, we can easily define tax investigation as a continuous process by tax authority or revenue department of recovering tax undercharged in previous years of assessment. Tax investigations will follow the same processes as normal audit investigation although the approach will be more on tax related issues. In this regard, tax investigation can take place where the taxpayer is suspected regarding to tax evasion, or just by random sampling in order to check whether these practices exist or do not exist.

The revenue authority has to conduct tax investigations not just by normal audit, as this might not be part of their mandate as stipulated in their engagement letter. Tax investigation success depends more on the capability of the staff of the revenue authority to detect all practices that are likely to cause under-collection of tax revenues. Tax investigation is an examination of taxpayer's business and / or individual books, records and documents. This examination is to ensure that the correct amount of income is reported and tax thereon paid in accordance to the tax laws and provisions. The investigation will only be carried out in cases where it is suspected based on precise and definite evidence that the taxpayer is deliberately trying to avoid paying tax or has committed an act of willful evasion under tax laws and other statutes.

Tax investigation activities act as a deterrent against tax evasion, ensure that the correct amount of tax is collected, ascertain the person responsible for the offence, pursue criminal prosecution and enhance voluntary compliance with tax laws and regulations.

11.2 IMPORTANCE OF TAX INVESTIGATION

Tax investigation becomes very important where the tax authority has gained knowledge about these important issues:

I. Taxpayer fails to lodge tax return. The reasons for non-filling of tax returns can be due to ignorance of taxpayers or willfully intention for non- submission.

II. Taxpayer fails to provide information requested by the tax authority. When the returns by the taxpayers do not contain the requested information by the revenue authority it may necessitate to carry out an investigation
III. Taxpayer submitted incorrect information to tax authority. Incorrect information conceals useful information for tax assessment.
IV. The corporation's auditor makes a qualified auditor report. Where a taxpayer submits qualified financial statements, it becomes an indicator of that there are might exists areas of tax fraud on financial affairs such that the revenue authority can carry on an investigation.
V. The tax return states an unreasonably low turnover, assessable income or profit percentage. When the revenue authority suspects that the taxpayer sales, income are higher than the one revealed by the returns it can entail to tax investigation
VI. Tax authority received report by a third party regarding the tax evasion. Sometimes, information about tax evasion and tax frauds are availed by third party, which becomes a starting point for tax revenue authority to carry on tax investigations.

11.3 CIRCUMSTANCES FOR TAX INVESTIGATIONS

All tax investigations are justifiable if there are certain indicators of tax mis-statement or under reporting. There many conditions or circumstances which may necessitate a tax investigation. The following are some of the conditions or circumstances that will necessitate to carry on an investigation.

- Benefits which could go un taxed
- Expenses could be overstated
- Invoices could be understated
- Management Remunerations
- Board Payments such sitting Allowances could be abnormal
- Related party transactions
- Indication of money laundering activities
- Observance of late filling of tax returns
- Frequent mistakes in the filling of tax returns
- Opening of offshore bank accounts could lead suspicion of tax evasion
- Involvement of high risk industry activities

11.4. CHALLENGES IN TAX INVESTIGATION

Successfully tax investigation is not easily achievable. There are many challenges that may impair the whole process. However, these challenges might not be the same from one country to another. The following are some of these challenges:

1. Lack of specialized skills among tax investigators
2. The low level of technology
3. Limited training facilities
4. Low level of computerization
5. Poor book keeping
6. High levels of corruption-poor morals
7. Lack of motivation by tax investigators
8. Low security on the investigators

11.5. INDICATORS OF INADEQUACY TAX INVESTIGATION

Tax investigation department under any revenue authority has a major role for all investigations related to tax evasion, avoidances or tax frauds. However, the inadequacy of the tax investigation department impairs its functions. The inadequacy of tax investigation department is evidenced by Very few cases of tax evasion that are successful prosecuted in court, Increased rate of illicit business activities, smuggling and Tax authority failure to meet revenue targets.

The causes of inadequacy are many including the following common causes:

- Not well staffed- Where the investigation department is understaffed it cannot manage to

cope with the huge workload of many investigation cases that include both small and big taxpayers whether they are individual or corporate taxpayers.
- Not well supported by management- In cases where management of the tax authority does not support the management, the department will not be able to function very well.
- Political interference- In some countries, political interference impairs the independence of tax auditors as they try to perform their work of investigation. This happens in cases where political leaders have major interests in those companies that are suspected of violating the tax laws of the country.
- Low levels of knowledge and skills
- Lack of teamwork within the staff
- Lack of co-operation from the public.
- Lack of motivation of Tax investigators
- Lack of morals
- Lack of computerized investigation systems
- High turnover of employees due to lack of morals
- Lack of specialized working facilities/equipment's eg Forensic lab

11.6. STREAMLINING TAX INVESTIGATION FUNCTION

Tax investigation function is important to enhance tax collection, minimize tax evasion and avoidances practices.

The use of variety efforts and strategies can streamline tax investigation functions. The following strategies can be useful in this case

   a. Governments need to ensure that the revenue authority have necessary legal power to conduct its activities without limitation and interference.eg power to prosecute tax cases
   b. Governments should enhance mutual agreement between different tax jurisdictions to facilitates tax investigation across borders
   c. Constitutional Immunity on tax administration to conduct their activities without political interference;
   d. Government can ensure that there is Internal mechanism to eliminate corruption within the Tax administration.
   e. Provide specialized training to tax investigators such as training in gas and oil
   f. Creating Public awareness on tax investigations
   g. Provide clear code of Ethics for the tax investigators
   h. Provide good remuneration of the tax investigators
   i. Provide security for tax investigators.

11.7. TAX INVESTIGATION FRAMEWORK

Tax investigation framework provides the road map on how the investigation has to be done. The objective of designing the framework is to ensure that all investigations are fair and transparent and at the same time it must give proper outline on the responsibilities of tax investigation officers, help them to carry out their tasks efficiently and effectively but at the same time, it should help the taxpayers to fulfil their obligations.

The key issues in the tax investigation framework should include the understanding of the statutory provisions, year of assessment as well as proper procedures on how to conduct tax investigations. Successfully investigation will also depend on the education, qualifications, experiences and exposures of the tax investigators. Knowledge in business, accounting, taxations and auditing could enhance the tax investigation function.

11.8. CONDUCTING TAX INVESTIGATION

Conducting tax investigation will reveal all irregulates and frauds on tax liability and it will help in recovering the amount of taxes that has been evaded through different illegal schemes. The investigation has to be structured in such a way that the investigators should be able to achieve its objectives. The following issues are important to consider during investigation exercise.

1. Understanding the Taxpayers entity
2. Identification of tax officials to do the investigation
3. Visit the taxpayer official premises
4. Explain the purpose of the visits to the taxpayer.

5. Conduct interview with taxpayers. The interview has to take place in the premises of the authority. Minutes has to be taken to authenticate that the meeting took place.
6. Request for Documentation and books for investigation
7. Consent to take documentation by the tax payers
8. Examination of records by the examination officer
9. Request for more information
10. Taxpayers can appoint a representative to act on behalf during the interview.
11. Agreement by both parties on tax liability
12. Finalization of tax investigation on the findings

11.9 WRITING TAX INVESTIGATION REPORT

Writing investigation report intends to inform senior tax official of what caused the undercharging of the tax income which was to be collected by the government. The investigator has to inform on his report the background of the investigated institution, the purpose and objectives of the investigation, scope and the methodology used in investigation. The investigation findings section has to have a clear methodology in order to give a clear picture of what was found in the investigation and conclusions from the findings. The investigator should give recommendations of the actions to be taken by senior tax official management as a follow up on all investigations findings.

SAMPLE TAX INVESTIGATION REPORT
AUDIT OF TAX EXEMPTIONS

To: General Commissioner
From: Director Legal Board Secretarial and Legal Services
Date: 20th September, 2017

RE: ABC TRUSTEES

1.0. BACKGROUND

The above-named beneficiary is registered under the Non-Government Organization regime with Certificate no 11 of 2016 and TIN Certificate no 102-909-860.The registered trustees is exempted under GN No 205 and 206 Of 2016. According to our systems the beneficiary has been granted tax exemption on sixteen (16) units of motor vehicles. (See appendix A). The beneficiary project is located on plot no 12 block Njiro area near ESAMI in Arusha municipal. The main activities of the Organization have been dealing with health and education.

2.0 OBJECTIVE

We are now doing verification on how the tax exempted goods have been granted to the beneficiary has been used properly and the existence of the project.

3.0 SCOPE

The verification on tax exempted goods was covered the period from 2016 to 2017.

4.0 METHODOLOGY

The investigation process was carried on by reviewing the documentations of the client, physical visit of the client premises, review of motor

(a) TRA System

We have gone through our systems I/Tax, Ascuda, and TANCIS, and found that the beneficiary has been granted on tax exemption on only sixteen (16) units of motor vehicles.

(b) Physical visit

We have visited the project site which is located to the above-named location, during the site visit we have found only six (6) units of vehicles, that the others vehicles are on duty. We further conducted the interview with the beneficiary's representative (see the interview attached

(c) Documents requested

In our effort to establish whether the beneficiary has been properly utilizing the tax-exempt vehicles, we request the beneficiary to submit the relevant documents.

(D) Motor vehicle registration cards

Out of sixteen (16) tax exempted motor vehicles, the beneficiary has submitted only eight (8) copies of cards.

(a) Log books
The log book submitted indicates that the routes of the vehicles are for the religious activities.

(b) Motor vehicle Insurance cover
The insurance cover submitted and related to the organization vehicles and all are valid.

(c) Motor vehicle service charges evidence
The receipts for service charges of motor vehicles submitted.

(d) Books of account (Financial statements)
The financial statement for the year 2016 was submitted and the vehicles indicating in the books as organization assets.

(e) Driver's employment contract
The contract was submitted then we were compared with the driving license and found are the same.

5) FINDING

In conducting verification of tax exemptions, we found that the trustee has been granted Tax exemption on sixteen (16) motor vehicles. (List of M/Vehicles is attached). Out of sixteen (16) tax exempted motor vehicles, the beneficiary has submitted only eight (8) copies of cards

We further called the beneficiary's representative in our office to give the explanation about the remaining registration cards and narrated that the vehicle was sold to non-tax exempted beneficiary. The motor vehicle whose registration cards are missing are attracting the duties amounting Ths. 231,518,391.80 (See Attachment No 2 the missing cards).

6) CONCLUTION

The duties and taxes of Tshs.231, 518,391.80 with respect to all vehicle be recovered

7) RECOMMENDATION

The tax exempted beneficiary should be educated how to handle the tax exempted goods.

Director Board Secretarial and Legal Services

PRACTICE QUESTIONS

Question 1

ABC Ltd is a company based in your country. The Company started business operation since 1971. The Company has a Business manager, assisted by the Chief accountant to manage business affairs of the company. Since then AXY Authorized Accountants and Auditor has been auditing the firm, the auditing firm has been issuing clean auditing reports all the times. However, recently the Revenue and Tax Authority conducted a tax investigation audit and came up with the report which created doubts as to whether auditing was conducted professionally. The Tax authority subjected the company to a tax liability of $300m due to non-tax compliance of various taxes over the past 5 Years. The report angered the company's board of directors and the board decided to change the auditors.

Discussion

a. Determine whether the decision of the board was correct
b. What do you think were the reasons for tax non-compliance?
c. What is your recommendation to ensure that the company is not experiencing the same problem in the future?

Question 2

What are the main reasons for tax investigation in any tax jurisdiction?

Question 3

What are likely to be challenges of Tax investigations in your country?

Question 4

What evidences are there to show the inadequacy of the tax investigation department in your country?

Question 5

How can the government streamline the tax investigation functions in your country?

Question 6

While conducting investigations which area do you think are critical for investigations and why?

Question 7

Which strategies/technique will you use to detect tax underreporting due to unreported income?

Question 8

Discuss how will you go about detecting tax underreported due to capitalization of business expenses?

12. WIDENING THE TAX BASE

❏ **Topic Objective**
The topic will help students to understand why widening the tax base is of highly importance to the government.

❏ **Coverage**
12.1 Introduction
12.2 Objectives of widening the tax base
12.3 Strategies for widening the tax base
12.4 Challenges of widening the tax base
Practice Questions

❏ **Learning Outcomes**
At the end of the topic, students should be able to understand how governments can design tax laws that can enhance the widening of the tax base

CHAPTER 12

Widening the Tax Base

12.1 INTRODUCTION

The crucial issues that face countries that face balance of payments deficits problem is how they can raise funds to curb deficits in their budget. From time to time, such countries would be thinking on how they can broaden their tax net to include more taxpayers in the tax net. This therefore may involve introducing more tax laws and amending the present laws that provide more loopholes for tax evasion and avoidances. However, this may not necessarily bring the expected results to the government. On the other side, it may have negative impact on economic productive sector if the new laws discourage both taxpayers and investors to engage themselves to productive activities, which are taxable. Therefore, widening tax base has to involve a carefully and purposefully study of the existing tax laws, the tax environment and possible new avenues that can help to bring a larger number of people in the tax base.

12.2 OBJECTIVES OF WIDENING THE TAX BASE

The objectives of widening the tax base are not so much different from the ones discussed above when discussing the objectives of tax reforms. However, we add few objectives below that are also in conformity with tax reforms objectives.

1. Widening the tax base could as the result of government desire to generate additional revenue in order to meet public development projects
2. Bridge down the deficit balance of payment in order to enhance the tax GDP ratio especially for countries that do experience problems with their balance of payments.
3. Bringing equality in tax jurisdiction. Over times government might discover that the tax net is not inclusive as it excludes certain groups of individuals from paying taxes which brings inequality among citizens. In order to avoid this practice, the government will design and implement a tax system that captures many individuals and entities in the tax net.

12.3 CHALLENGES IN ENHANCING THE TAX BASE

Enhancing the tax base is a key factor for increased revenue for the government. The wider the tax base the greater the opportunity for generating more funds to meet public expenditures. Therefore, designing strategies to enhance the tax base should be a continuous process that has to be done from year to year. There are always challenges in enhancing the tax base in the whole process. The challenges are many caused by various reasons. One of the challenges arises from the fact the informal sector has so many activities that are not easily captured by the tax systems and its difficulty to incorporate all the activities because of inadequate or weak systems to capture potential taxpayers' information.

There is also a lot of political interference when trying to capture the informal sector into tax net. Political leaders use the informal sector platform to gain their political influence such that they may not want certain groups of individuals not to be taxed. In some countries corruption is so high that it impairs all activities to tax certain businesses or individuals. High tax administration costs, weak tax administration also impairs the efforts to widen the tax base, while resistance to change due to High illiteracy level on issues of taxation also impairs efforts to widen the tax base.

Countries that are likely to widen their tax bases are the ones which embrace venturing in new areas of revenue generation but long, bureaucratic and complex decision-making process to adopt new challenges and low physical planning can bring stagnation to expanding the tax base. This challenge is more magnified if there is Challenges due to low levels of tax knowledge by tax officials and weak regulatory framework.

In developing countries technology level may stagnate the growth of the tax bases. Low integration of information technology will create room for tax evasion and avoidance by MNC hence difficulties in collecting the right amount of taxes and difficulties of taping into the hidden sector.

12.4. STRATEGIES TO WIDEN THE TAX BASE

Apart from the challenges discussed above there is still a room for any government to apply different strategies to overcome those challenges in widening its tax base. The strategies can be applied together or individually depending on prevailing tax base already in place. These strategies are not all inclusive to address the need for widening as more strategies are likely to be devised. We mention blow the following strategies. The following strategies seem to be the most common strategies that various countries in African countries as well as other developing and developed countries have used to widen their tax bases in order to achieve the tax objectives in their countries. The extents to which these strategies have been applied vary from one country to another.

i. Integration of technology in the tax structures e.g. use of electronic devices for enhancing tax compliance and collection, government can also give subsidies so that businesses can afford these devices.

ii. Improvement in business registration so as to increase the number of possible tax payers and hence widen the tax base
iii. Application of strategies to attract more Foreign Direct Investment (FDI) and this will enhance the corporate tax through increased business and increased PAYE.
iv. Inclusion of more sectors in the tax system that were previously not remitting taxes e.g. Real estate
v. Invest in taxpayer education to create awareness and importance of taxation to economic development. This also enhances voluntary compliance by taxpayers
vi. Introduction of presumptive tax (mostly in informal sectors) where returns are very low.
vii. Encouraging local production of goods. This will enhance the tax base
viii. Review of legislation on tax exemptions which can lead to the removal or reduction of too many tax exemptions
ix. Investment in e-commerce technology and e-taxation

12.5 POTENTIAL AREAS FOR WIDENING TAX BASES

The potential for widening the tax base of a country depends so much on the country economic base, its location and comparative advantage which it enjoys apart from other countries. Countries with higher comparative advantage are likely to have more economic activities leading them to have a higher potential of growth in their tax bases. Countries with more natural resources are also likely to have higher potential of growing their agricultural and mining and tourism sectors sector which is an opportunity to widen the tax base. In some other countries the informal sector has potential of growth hence creating much room for increasing the tax base though taping taxes from the informal sector is a big challenge for many developing countries.

The growth of telecommunication sector in developing countries as the results of multinational companies investing in these countries gives opportunity to create a room for widening the tax base. Potential Avenues to expand their tax bases as there will be more agriculture and mining activities.

12.6. POTENTIAL AREAS FOR WIDENING TAX BASE IN AFRICAN COUNTRIES

In order to increase the tax base, a country should avoid the problem of relying on few sources of incomes. Majority of African countries have narrow tax bases but there are number of potential economic sectors to explore more which include the following areas

- Agriculture
- Mining/oil/gas

- Telecommunications
- Tourism
- Informal sector
- Manufacturing
- Financial sector
- Insurance sector.

12.7 POTENTIALITY OF THE INFORMAL SECTOR IN TAX REVENUE GENERATION

The informal sector has a lot of economic activities that generate a lot of money which go untaxed causing the government not to collect taxes. Despite the fact that the activities in the informal sector are considered to be less profitable it is not always true that the sector does not generate income which cannot be subjected to tax. There is high potential for governments to collect taxes from the informal sector despite of the following challenges:

i. Political issues i.e. lack of political goodwill to enable legislation to guide the inclusion of some entities in the informal sector into the tax system.
ii. The informal sector has so many unstructured types of businesses.
iii. There is difficulty of capturing data about the sector activities Limiting data or lack of a data base on the informal sector.
iv. Lack of adequate capacity in the Revenue Authority to

v. Poor infrastructure to the location of most businesses in the informal sector i.e. in the rural areas.
vi. High administration costs
vii. Lack of a legal framework on the taxation of the informal sector.
viii. Legal framework failing to capture the sector
ix. Poor recordkeeping.
x. weak tax knowledge resulting in poor tax compliance
xi. Low value of economic activities.
xii. Poor understanding & monitoring by tax authorities.

12.8. WIDENING THE TAX BASE IN THE DIGITAL ECONOMY

In the last twenty years we have seen an exponential growth in technology which has resulted to change in how business is done in world we live today. Cross border business and international payments systems has been made much easier and faster. The development of digitized economy creates a major gap on how taxation of business has to be done especially in developing countries.

Multinationals corporations operating in these developing countries are taking advantage by avoiding and evading taxes as developing countries are still lagging behind in addressing taxation in digitized economy where traditional tax laws, procedures and systems cannot easily cope with the pace of operations in the modern economy. This results to inability of countries to expand their tax base in order to collect more taxes to meet their public expenditures. Only developed countries have realized the need to shift from the traditional tax laws in order to cope with the pace.

Developing countries need to come up with inclusive structure tax structure and systems to address these challenges. Challenges of widening the tax base in digitized economy have positive impact of increasing tax evasion by Multinationals Companies. Developing countries infrastructure and capacity building of local staff is still low and not capable of addressing the challenges of taxation in digitized economies.

Introduction of block chain technology and usage of new crypto currency such as bit coins in international business payment transaction is changing how business is done in the modern world which also affects taxation of businesses and it is likely to impact the tax collection of countries which have no proper technology infrastructure and human capacity to address these new developments. In other words, the exponential growth of new technological development is not supported with proper governance, regulations and taxation laws in most developing countries to support tax collection from e-transactions. It is important.

PRACTICE QUESTIONS

Question 1

What specific strategies that have been undertaken by member countries in East African countries to widen the tax base over the past decade?

Question 2

What challenges/weaknesses are likely to be experienced by African countries as they try to enhance their tax bases?

Question 3

What strategies should be used by these countries to increase the tax base in the future?

Question 4

Which sectors of African countries have greater potential for widening the tax base?

Question 5

Why the informal sector in Africa generates fewer revenues in terms of taxation?

13. TAX EXEMPTIONS

❑ **Topic Objectives**
Introduce students to Tax Exemptions

❑ **Coverage**
13.1. Introduction
13.2. Challenges in Tax Exemption
13.3. Enhancing Tax Exemptions
Practice Questions

❑ **Learning Outcomes**
Students will be able to understand the why tax exemptions are important and how to mitigate tax exemptions abuse.

CHAPTER 13

Tax Exmption

13.1. INTRODUCTION

Tax exemption is completely full remission or reduction of tax liability to certain individuals or corporate entities. All exempted individuals or corporate entities especially the non –profit organizations that receive the exemption will not require paying taxes. However, all taxes revenue exempted reduces the government revenues. On the side of the government tax exemption reduces the tax revenues. Despite these losses governments still pursue the option because of other objectives. The objective of granting these exemptions is to give a tax relief to the recipient and in some cases to encourage certain types of investment in a given sector. Tax exemptions aims at reducing or tax liability When tax exemption is granted, the recipient is expected to use the exemption for the aim of providing public services which are not catered under the government budget.

The reasons for grating tax exemptions to individuals and corporate may vary but generally governments will consider giving these exemptions to diplomats in order to benchmark with international standards. One should also note that tax exemptions are permissible by law. It means that before exemptions are granted or claimed a law is needed to identify which categories of individuals, organizations or products are exempt from taxes. Once in place, these privileges are hard to revoke as the beneficiaries are likely to lobby for their continuity.

Majority of African countries provide tax exemptions for various reasons explained above. They also dedicate to management of these exemptions in order to minimize the abuse. Management of tax exemptions requires an exemption unit for proper organization structure to administer the exemption. Such department might be involved in Submitting tax exemption reports to treasury on monthly basis, verification and monitoring of customs duties exemptions on importation of vehicles by public officials, verification and monitoring of VAT exemptions on NGOs and Religious Institutions, verification and monitoring of exemptions issued through TIC certificates of incentives and other schemes and Advising on exemption administration.

13.2. CHALLENGES IN TAX EXEMPTIONS

All tax exemptions are likely to excessive or prone to abuse. The following are the major challenges in all granting tax exemptions

1. Weak tax laws on exemptions that create loopholes for granting excessive exemptions hence providing a room for increased tax avoidances practices.
2. Collusion of tax officials with tax payers on granting the tax exemptions. Tax officials have been teaching the taxpayers on the weaknesses of the tax laws.
3. Political interference on granting tax exemptions. In some cases, political leaders have interfered decisions by Revenue Authorities on granting these exemptions by forcing tax authorities to grant exemptions to non-qualifiers
4. Abuses of the exemptions by the beneficiaries. Beneficiaries have bought goods above what was permissible and claimed exemptions
5. Use of forged documents to obtain tax exemptions
6. Shortage number of staff to administer, monitor, verification and control by the revenue authorities poses challenges in administering exemptions.
7. Unfettered discretionary tax exemption by minister leads to enjoyment of tax exemption by unqualified beneficiaries and therefore unfair tax exemption granted on social relation basis rather than merit.
8. Existence of administrative tax exemption that are not prescribed under the law poses an enforcement challenges in cases of abuse.

13.3. ENHANCING TAX EXEMPTIONS

It is not possible to exclude all tax exemptions in any tax regimes. Tax exemptions have to continually given to entitled individuals, groups and other nonprofit organizations. However, can must be exercised in order to minimize the abuse, avoid granting the exemptions to non-qualifier as well as grating excessive exemptions. Therefore, it is important to take into consideration a number of strategies if at all tax exemption has to remain productive such as the following:

1. Review of the tax laws which permit loopholes to grant excessive tax exemptions. A comprehensive review of all tax exemptions under different laws is important so as to understand the benefit and costs.
2. All tax exemptions should be strict provided under the law
3. Getting rid of discretionary exemptions by the minister of commissioner of the revenue authorities. In this case the introduction of statutory guidelines to guide the minister or commissioner when providing discretionary exemptions becomes important.
4. Strengthen the enforcement laws on audit and verification
5. Improving government accountability and transparency on all matters pertaining to tax investigations will help to minimize the abuses of tax exemptions and reduce powers of individuals on granting discretionary exemptions.

PRACTICE QUESTIONS

Question 1

Tax exemption is like a desert: it is good to have but it does not help very if the meal is not there". Discuss this statement in context of justification on non-justification of tax exemption existence.

Question 2

What are the main objectives of granting tax exemptions?

Question 3

Discuss how tax exemptions is managed in your own country.

Question 4

Establish the detailed exemptions under each of the following tax laws in VAT Act, Income Tax Act, Property tax and Customs Management Act.

Question 5

What conditions or criteria are used for granting exemptions in each of the above category?

14. FOREIGN DEBT

❏ **Topic Objectives**
Introduce students to foreign debts concept

❏ **Coverage**
14.1. Introduction
14.2. Categories of external debts
14.3. Magnitude of external debt and its impact
14.4. Management of external debts
14.5. Strategies to reduce external debts
14.6. Developing countries support in reducing African countries debts
Practice Questions

❏ **Learning Outcomes**
Students will be able to understand the role of external debts in African countries economies

CHAPTER 14

Foreign Debt

14.1 INTRODUCTION

In modern economies business organizations do finance their business operations by using their own equities and debts. This is not different on how governments finance their operating and capital expenditures. Most government does finance their expenditures by obtaining loans from other foreign governments and international organizations. Even developed countries do borrow funds from international financial institutions to finance their budgets for public expenditures. Developing countries mostly African countries are highly indebted because a greater percentage of their budgets are financed by foreign debts, which attract high interest rates and payable in long term of period. The magnitude of foreign debts by developing countries is very high as compared to developed countries.

Foreign debts bear high interest rates, which continue making the debt magnitude high instead of going down. Developing countries subsistence economies do not help them to reduce these debts as the production capacity is still very low due to various factors that affect these economies. Despite the fact that there have been times where developed countries have been giving debt relief to these countries, these counties have continued to borrow largely to support their deficit balance of payments. By looking at various statistics of for example African countries debts, the debts have been increasing over the last decade.

14.2 CATEGORIES OF EXTERNAL DEBTS

External debts classification includes bilateral debts, multilateral debts and commercial debts.

a. **Bilateral Debts**

These are external debts granted by individual country to another country. Rich countries, which are member of the Paris Club, are the ones, which grant such types of debts. Countries that have offered such loans to African countries include Austria, Belgium, Canada, France, Germany, Italy, Norway, United States of America, United Kingdom and the Netherlands both of them are members of the Paris club. Non-Paris club member countries also grant bilateral debts to African countries, such as Russia, Bulgaria, India, Kuwait, China, Libya, Hungary and many others.

b. **Multilateral Debts**

External debts granted to individual countries by multilateral institutions. These institutions include the World Bank, African Development Bank (AFDB), International Monetary Fund (IMF), and International Fund for Agriculture Development (IFAD), European Investment Bank (EIB) and the Nordic Development Fund (NORDF).

c. **Commercial Loans**

These are loans borrowed mostly by private companies from the international financial institutions and commercial banks and other creditors abroad. They are normally non-concessional since borrowing is at the market interest rates. Examples of international financial institutions offering such types of loans include the International Financial Corporation (IFC).

14.3. MAGNITUDE OF THE EXTERNAL DEBT

The magnitude of developing countries external debt is very huge. The increasing external debt in Africa is mainly for financing balance of payments deficit. According to statistics availed by the World Bank, Sub-Saharan African countries for example receive $10 billion in aid but loses $14 billion in debt payments per year. Despite the fact that there have been reliefs given to African Countries by donor countries, the magnitude of debts has never gone down but it has continued to increase as African countries still have challenges that impair economic productive capacity.

Loan servicing by African countries for example have negative impact on economic development and health support as they divert resources from HIV/AIDS programs, education and other important needs. Although African countries have been campaigning for debt cancelations by developed countries, the U.S. and other rich countries have resisted calls to cancel these debts, instead proposing partial solutions that are inadequate and impose harsh economic policies on indebted countries.

The impact of high debts differs from one country to another. Looking at statistics for example for different African Countries, while more than 80 million Nigerians live on less than $1 per day, in 2005 Nigeria agreed to pay over $12 billion to the Paris Club of creditors in exchange for partial debt cancellation. In 2003, Zambia spent twice as much on debt repayments as on health care. Nevertheless, partial debt cancellation allowed the government to grant free basic healthcare to its population in 2006. It is very clear that serving of external debt is a greater burden to developing Countries economic and social development.

14.4. MANAGEMENT OF DEBTS

Management of foreign debts in developing countries faces many challenges. These challenges continue making these countries increase their foreign debts as a big way for supporting their balance of payments deficits. The following challenges are common among developing countries;

a. Fluctuating Interest rates

Interest rates on loans fluctuate and this increases the burden of debts. Since these debts are repayable in a longer period, there is greater room for escalating the interest rates thus making the debts un-payable.

b. Oil Global Prices

Changes in global oil price, which have tremendous effect on production costs and economy growth. Most African countries do not produce oil and they have to import oil from producing countries. Most African countries spend high part of their foreign exchange budget in buying fuel, which affects the foreign exchange reserves. When foreign exchange reserves are not enough, serving foreign debts becomes difficulty.

c. Misappropriation and embezzlements

Miss-management of funds in developing countries is very common due to high level of corruption. There are cases of funds misappropriation and embezzlements by corrupt leaders in some countries including those funds, obtained through foreign debts.

d. Global financial crisis on developing economies

There have been a number of global economic crises, which have affected developing countries' economies to such extent that African countries are not able to raise enough foreign exchange to pay their foreign debts.

Consider for example the case of the 2009 financial global crisis, which affected the tourism sector and agriculture sector, which at the end affected the capacity to generate foreign exchanges.

e. Climate Changes

Climate Changes affects the agricultural sector, which is the economic base for most developing countries. The climate changes affect the countries' economies. Droughts and floods had tremendously affected the agriculture sector, which is the backbone of many African countries. Where agricultural sector is affected, the available foreign exchange is used for importation of foods and nothing remains for payment of foreign debts.

f. Anti-Competitive Policies

Anti-competitive policies by developing countries which impair African efforts to boost their cash inflows through exports- While African countries are trying hard to boost their production capacity that is aimed at increasing their exports, developing countries on the other hand are putting barriers by using anti-competitive policies against products originating from African countries.

14.5 STRATEGIES TO REDUCE FOREIGN DEBT

The increasing external debts burden is an obstacle for African countries development. African countries should reduce their external debts by using a combination of various strategies that are likely to reduce the burden. The elimination of the debts completely is not possible even though there are number of debt reliefs programs, which have been availed. African countries have continued borrowing even after receiving the relief. Reducing the debts requires a combination of strategies to include the following;

1. NEGOTIATION FOR REDUCED INTEREST RATES

African countries could involve in negotiations with donor countries on reduced interest rates or waiver of interest rates. This is possible as now there are typical examples of international Organization that are offering loans to developing countries at lower rates. A typical example is with the World Bank, which in the last two years it has been offering loans at lower interest rates.

2. NEGOTIATION ON WAIVER OF ADVANCED DEBTS

African countries should continue their negotiations with the rich countries on the full waiver of external debts despite the fact that these countries do not want to give 100% waiver. These countries insist on partial solutions that are inadequate and impose harsh economic policies on indebted countries. African countries should continue putting pressure on complete waiver of the loans.

2. USE OF EXEMPTED FUNDS FOR DEVELOPING ECONOMIC SECTOR GROWTH

Another strategy for African countries is to utilize the exempted funds for developing economic sectors that will help to boost the foreign exchange earnings capacity through export of manufactured goods and food production. Enhancing African countries capacities to earn foreign exchange will help to generate enough funds to service their external debts.

4. CONVERTING SOME LOANS TO EQUITY

Conversion of long term loans to equity can another strategy to reduce debts of companies/institutions. This strategy requires companies to seek negotiations with the financing international organizations. This means that if the financing organizations are willing to convert their loans to equity it means they become shareholders in the company.

5. EXTENSION OF LOAN REPAYMENT PERIOD:

Countries can negotiate for extension of loan repayment period. This gives advtanges to a country in times where the economic performance is poor. However, in some cases where the agreement for extension do not waiver interest rates escalations it may be very costly in future as interest will continue increasing hence creating more burden in term of servicing the loan.

6. GOVERNMENT PRIORITIES IN SPENDING PUBLIC FUNDS

African countries should have priority spending of money obtained through loans by directing the funds to foreign exchange generating projects.

14.6 DEVELOPING COUNTRIES SUPPORT FOR REDUCING AFRICAN DEBTS

There have been number of efforts by developing countries and International organization in reducing African debts at individual country. Developed countries have been giving waiver to African countries from time to time. The waiver is on country-to-country basis after fulfilling the required conditions before granting the waiver. These waiver initiatives have helped African countries to reduce their debt service obligations and direct the debt relief savings to financing priority sectors including health, primary education, water, agriculture and rural roads. The waiver has helped to reduce the debt service to manageable levels without crowding out priority spending.

Debt reliefs have brought significant changes to recipient countries. Tanzania, as one of the countries that has benefited from debts relief, used savings from debt relief, averaging US$ 80 million a year to import vital food for those affected by drought and increased education spending and removing the primary school fees.

Uganda is another country, which used the debt relief to fund for UPE, fight HIV and provide clean water. Other countries, which used the debt reliefs effectively, include Mozambique, Ghana, Cameroon, and Burundi. These countries directed the debts relief savings into vaccination programmes, infrastructure development, education programme and other social services. The following are international association that have supported African countries efforts to eliminate or reduce the external debt.

THE PARIS CLUB

One of the international associations of creditors that have been supporting African countries in debt relief is the Paris Club. The Paris club is comprised of group of 19 rich countries formed for the aim of providing financial services such as debt restructuring and debts cancellation to indebted countries. Countries, which benefited are those recommended by the International Monetary Fund after meeting certain conditions. The permanent member nations of the club are United States of America, United Kingdom, Sweden, Spain, Italy, Ireland, Germany, France, Finland, Denmark, Canada, Belgium, Austria, Australia, Japan, Netherlands, Norway, Russia and Switzerland.

The efforts to support heavily indebted countries (HIPCs) which include most African countries were supportive in the beginning of the early nineties. In 1990, there were larger amount of debt cancellations to these countries. These numbers of options were available to HIPC'S as far as their debts are concerned;

1. Longer repayment periods-Normal repayment was ten years with one-year grace period. However, poor countries can now benefit more for a longer period of repayment under special arrangement. The maximum repayment period is now 23 years (including 6 years of grace period) for commercial loans and 40 years (including 16 years of grace period) for official development aid loans.
2. Completely debt cancellation- The Paris club for example on 15th Sept 2009 cancelled about $ 53.6 million to the Central Africa Republic, which was almost 6% of the Central Africa External debt.
3. Special treatment based on individual cases- At the same time, the Paris club has special treatment for countries experiencing major catastrophes and major problems caused by political conflicts and instability. In case of natural catastrophes, Paris club grants an option for debt deferrals of all payments on debt services for a certain period. Where countries' economies are affected by long-standing internal political conflicts., the Paris Club can go beyond usual terms by granting for instance, a three-year deferral of all debt service payments.

NON-PARIS CLUB COUNTRIES

These countries lend bilateral loans similar to ones, which are given can by Paris Club member countries. They have also provided debt reliefs to African countries in line with the ones, which HIPC programme of the Paris club. Examples of such countries include Bulgaria, India, Kuwait, China, Hungary, and Libya. These countries, which give bilateral loans, they are more advance than most of the African countries. African countries can continue strengthening the economic relationship with these countries so that they can continue negotiations on debt reductions and retirement of their debt via debt for equity swap, debt for natural resources, debt for aid or other local currency swaps in manner that can benefit their economies and reducing the country's debt.

PRACTICE QUESTIONS

Question 1

What are the main challenges in managing external debts in developing countries?

Question 2

What strategies are available for developing countries in reducing the external debt?

Question 3

Discuss the relevance of external debts to African economies development.

Question 4

Discuss how the Paris club is involved in supporting African countries to reduce their external debts.

15. BALANCE OF PAYMENTS

❏ **Topic Objectives**
Introduce the students on knowledge of balance of payments.

❏ **Coverage**
15.1. Introduction
15.2. Balance of Payment
15.3. Components of Balance of Payment
15.4. Narrative Format of Balance of Payments
15.5. Balance of payments challenges in developing countries and strategies mitigation
15.6. Promoting invisible trade in developing countries
Practice Questions

❏ **Learning Outcomes**
Students will be able to understand how to compute the balance of payment of a country and understand which factors influence the balance of payments.

CHAPTER 15

Balance of Payments

15.1 INTRODUCTION

One way in which a country can account for the economic activities taking place in a country is through use of national accounting whereby a country considers its aggregate supply and its aggregate demand. The aggregate supply refers to the amount of output (goods & services) the economy can produce in a given period, normally one year taking into consideration of the technology and resources available in a country while aggregate demand refers to the total demand of goods and services for consumption, investment and purchase by government and for exports. The aggregate supply is also, referred as the gross domestic product (GDP) which refers to the output of goods and services produced in the economy in a given period. The GDP does not include foreign payments, net funds arising from outside the country.

When payments from abroad are added to GDP, you obtain the result is the Gross National Product. However, what is captured in national accounting is not inclusive of all economic activities in a country as the informal sector has always remained out of the basket when national accounting data are captured.

15.2 BALANCE OF PAYMENTS

Balance of payment is another approach which gives quantitative explanation of economic transaction taking place in a country for a given period time. We can therefore define balance of payments as a summary of flows of economic transactions between residents of one country and foreign countries during a given period, normally a year (one year). Other words that can explain balance of payments are the ones which state that the balance of payment as a system of recording all payments and receipts related to all economic activities carried by individuals, governments, private sector that are taking place within the country and ones taking place between a nation and foreign countries. Balance of payments accounting also faces the same challenges of not being able to capture all economic activities as experienced with the national accounting approach.

15.3 COMPONENTS OF THE BALANCE OF PAYMENTS

Balance of payments has the following three major components. These components include the current account, official reserve and the current account. When these components are put together they make the overall balance of payments of the country. The overall balance of payment can be negative or positive.

A. CURRENT ACCOUNT

This comprises of international transactions between a country with other countries that involve imports and exports of goods and services as well as private transfer that take place between the country and other countries. The current account has three main components;

(i) Visible trade balance

This is the difference between total value of exports and imports of goods. The difference can either be positive or negative. Where exports value is higher than imports value then we have positive visible trade balance. Where exports are less than imports then there is deficit visible trade. In most developing countries, especially African countries, their visible trade is always negative because of higher import bill but less exports.

(ii) Invisible trade Balance

This is the difference between total value of service payments (imports) and total value of service receipts (exports). Where the country provides services to another country means it is exporting and where a country receives services from another country then it is importing. Again, developing countries do have a challenge of having negative invisible trade balance as value of service receipts tend to be lower than value of service payments.

(iii) Private Transfers

B. OFFICIAL RESERVE ACCOUNT

This comprises of gold reserves, foreign exchange reserves, special drawings rights (SDR's) and reserve position in the International Monetary Fund (IMF)

C. CAPITAL ACCOUNT

This comprises of long term funds flow of capital nature between a country and another country. Capital accounts is comprised of

1. Foreign direct investments. This includes all financial assets resulting from net direct investments.
2. Portfolio Investments- This is in the form of equity and debt securities such as official loans and private loans
3. Other short-term investments such as purchase and sale of short term financial assets

15.4. NARATIVE FORMAT OF BALANCE OF PAYMENTS

Balance of Payments – Year xxx

1	+ Export Value of goods	X1
2	- Import Value of goods	X2
3	=Visible trade balance	X3
4	+ Service Receipts	Y1
5	-Service Payments	Y2
6	=Invisible trade Balance	Y3
7	=Overall Trade Balance (X3+Y3)	Z1
8	+ Private Transfers	X4
9	= Current Account Balance ((Z1+ X4)	Z2
10	OFFICIAL RESERVE ACCOUNT	
11	+Official Transfers (grants, tech assistance., program assistance, food aid)	X5
12	CAPITAL ACCOUNT	
13	+/- Capital Accounts (official loans- IBRD, IDA, Bilateral; Private capital- loans, FDI's; Foreign loan amort. +interest	X6
14	**=OVERALL BALANCE OF PAYMENTS (Z2+X5+X6)**	**BP**

Example 1

The following information is a summary of data for a hypothetical country ZM. Use this information to answer the questions that follow. Assume that this all the basic data that is available.

1. GDP at Market Prices = $3500
2. Imports FOB = $1250
3. Exports FOB = *Q = 40; P = $25/unit
4. Imports CIF = 120% of Imports f.o.b.
5. Service Payments (Interest, Insurance, etc.) = $50
6. Service Receipts (Tourism, etc.) = $25
7. Private Transfers = $30
8. Official Transfers = $120
9. Private capital inflows = $125
10. External Loan Amortization = $75
11. External Reserves (previous period) = $800
12. Reserve Requirements (minimum) = 8 months of imports C.I.F
13. Exchange Rate = 1:1
14. Corporate Income (Estimate) = $800
15. Domestic Debt = $600

Required

Determine the balance of payments status of this country

Solution

Exports FOB	$ 1000
Imports FOB	$ (1250)
Visible Trade Balance	$ (250)
Service Receipts	$50
Service Payments	($300)
	$ (275)
Invisible Balance	$(525)
Private Transfers	30
Current A/C Balance	$(495)
Official Transfers	120
Current A/c including official transfers	$(375)
Capital A/C transactions	
Private Capital inflows	$125
External Loan Amortization	75
	$ 50
Net Balance	$(325)

Reserves B/F $800
New Reserve Balance $475
Required Reserves $1000 (8 months imports CIF)
Reserves Short $525
Additional reserve needs $525*
(* Balance of payments support basis)

15.5. BALANCE OF PAYMENTS CHALLENGES IN DEVELOPING COUNTRIES

Most developing countries especially African countries do experience deficit balance of payment as the result of persistent various economic and social factors. They include the following factors

1. Low level of industrialization, which leads to inability to produce enough products for exports, causing inability to generate enough foreign exchange to finance the budget. At the same time even, the products produced by the existing industry have a challenge of competition in the world market due to low quality and high cost of production. African countries should focus on industrialization in order to boost exports in order to boost foreign exchange earnings.
2. African countries exports are more on unprocessed products which do not have higher value as processed products which can high prices in the market and be able to generate enough foreign exchange. African countries rely on substance economies, production of food and less for exports. African countries should support the growth of small industries that can add value to raw products instead of exporting unprocessed products.
3. In some African countries the political instability leads to low production of goods to export as

political havoc disturbs peace and harmony which is the key for human capital employment in the production process.
4. African investment climate is not conducive for investment growth as there is no priority focus on investments; policies are not conducive to attract foreign investment. More reforms in fiscal and monetary policies are needed in order to attract foreign investment in African countries.
5. In some African countries the legal framework is unfavorable for both local and foreign investment. Too much restriction in business licensing and corruption inhibit investments growth which is can help the country to increase its earnings.
6. African countries have challenges of inadequate and poor infrastructure. Poor roads, airports, inadequate power generations, small ports and other facilities are key setbacks for production of goods, services and trade facilitation in the continent. Where production level is low and trade volume is low, countries will always experience a deficit balance of payment.
7. The population growth rate in Africa is very high as compared to economic and production growth such that addressing health issues, education, securities and other peoples need requires a lot of funds which is not available. This leads to deficit balance of payments.
8. The impact of HIV/AIDS, malaria on African population reduces production capacities as more

resources are consumed to address these problems. More efforts are needed to manage and reduce HIV infections.

15.6 PROMOTING INVISIBLE TRADE IN DEVELOPING COUNTRIES

Invisible trade is the difference between services receipts and services payments. In developing countries, the overall balance of trade is always negative; the same applies to the invisible trade balance. African service exports to foreign countries are very low as compared to services imports from developed countries. The deficit invisible trade is due to various reasons including the followings

1. Shortage number of intellectuals and brain drainage
2. Limited number of academic institutions
3. Lack of modern technology for training
4. Altitude of government of using consultants from foreign countries and ignoring local consultants
5. Lack of skilled manpower to send abroad due to low quality of education and weak education systems. Local experts are considered of a low quality.
6. Low investment in research, innovation and development which leads to lack of professionals.
7. Low level of budget allocation to education
8. Donor restrictions on use of foreign consultants, example is on road construction projects where donors insist the use of specific foreign consultants.

PRACTICE QUESTIONS

Question 1

The Balance of Payment of African Countries has been declining over the past ten years ago at a higher rate. Discuss what reasons are for the decline and what recommendations are you making to improve the situation.

Question 2

What are the negative effects of African Countries dependence on foreign aids to finance their deficit balance of payments?

Question 3

What are the impairing factors in improving invisible trade balance in Africa and what can be done by can African Countries do to improve their invisible trade balance?

Question 4

African import bill is very high as compared to developed countries. What are likely to be the reasons and what can be done to reduce the import bill?

Question 5

What are the inefficiency of using the Gross Domestic Product as an economic and welfare indicator?

Bibliography

1. Aguolu, Osita (1999), Taxation and tax management in Nigeria, Enugu, Meridian Associates.\
2. Alm, j., Mclelland G. & W. D. Schulze 1992. Why do people pay taxes? *Journal of Public Economics, 48, 21-38.*
3. Azizul I (2001) Issues in Tax Reforms: Asia Pacific Development Journal Vol 1
4. Bird, Richard. 1983. 'Income tax reform in developing countries: The administrative dimension', (pp. 3-14) in International Bulletin of Fiscal Documentation, Vol. 37. International Bureau of Fiscal Documentation
5. Cowell, F. and Gordon F. (1988). *Unwillingness to pay: Tax evasion and public good provision. Journal of Public Economics 36, 305-321*
6. Devas N, Deky S and Hubbard M. (2001). Revenue Authorities: Are they vehicles for improved vehicles for improved tax administration Public Administration and Development 21: 211-222
7. East Africa Community Management Act 2006
8. Export Processing Zone Act 2006
9. Fabrizio Ferrari & Ricardo Rolfin **(2008)** investing in a Dangerous World: A New Political Risk Index
10. González Cano, J. 1996. *Armonización Tributaria del Mercosur. Buenos Aires: Instituto Universitario de Finanzas Públicas Argentinas.*
11. Government of Tanzania, Income Tax Act 2004
12. Government of Tanzania, Value Added Tax Act 2006

13. Hamada J., Haugerudbraaten H., Hickman A., Khaykin I. (2004), *Country and Political Risk. Practical Insights for Global Finances*, S. Wilkins, Risk Books
14. Harry M. Kitlya (2011) Tax Administrative Reforms in Tanzania- Experiences and Challenges-Conference Paper on Revenue Mobilization in Developing countries-IFM Fiscal Affair- Washington D.C
15. International Monetary Fund, 2005 "International Financial Statistic March 2005
16. Investment Promotion Act no. 6 of 2004 Sessional paper No. 2 of 19 on small Enterprise and Jua Kali Development in Kenya.
17. Jackson, B. R., & Million, V. C. (1986). Tax compliance research: Findings, problems, and prospects. *Journal of Accounting Literature*, 5 (1), 25-65.
18. Jonathan Di John (2006): The political Economy of Taxation and Tax reforms in developing countries. United Nations University, Research paper No 76, pp 1-27
19. Kasaro and Kiria (2009), Tax Incentives. *The Accountant. Journal of the National board of Accounts and Auditors Tanzania, Volume 24 Issue*
20. Kichler, E., E. Hoelzl & I. Wahl 2008. Enforced versus voluntary tax compliance: The "slippery slope" framework. Journal of Economic Psychology, 29, 210-225.
21. Krugman, Paul (1979). "A model of Balance of Payments Crises." Journal of Money, Credit, and Banking, 11, 311-25.
22. Lekinyi N. Mollel (2009), *Impact of Debt Relief on Fiscal Allocation to Priority Social Sectors and Response of Social Indicators in the HIPCS: A Case study of Tanzania*
23. Lekinyi N. Mollel (2009), *private sector External Debt Management Tanzania, Paper presented at sensitization seminar on commercial banks on the importance of private sector external debt.*
24. Levin, J. (2009) Taxation in Tanzania – Revenue Performances and Incidents Country Economic Report 2005, Sida, Helniski.
25. Lise Rakner and Sari Gloppen (2002). Tax Reforms and Democratic Accountability in Sub- Sahara Africa

Bibliography

1. Aguolu, Osita (1999), Taxation and tax management in Nigeria, Enugu, Meridian Associates.\
2. Alm, j., Mclelland G. & W. D. Schulze 1992. Why do people pay taxes? *Journal of Public Economics, 48, 21-38.*
3. Azizul I (2001) Issues in Tax Reforms: Asia Pacific Development Journal Vol 1
4. Bird, Richard. 1983. 'Income tax reform in developing countries: The administrative dimension', (pp. 3-14) in International Bulletin of Fiscal Documentation, Vol. 37. International Bureau of Fiscal Documentation
5. Cowell, F. and Gordon F. (1988). *Unwillingness to pay: Tax evasion and public good provision. Journal of Public Economics 36, 305-321*
6. Devas N, Deky S and Hubbard M. (2001). Revenue Authorities: Are they vehicles for improved vehicles for improved tax administration Public Administration and Development 21: 211-222
7. East Africa Community Management Act 2006
8. Export Processing Zone Act 2006
9. Fabrizio Ferrari & Ricardo Rolfin **(2008)** investing in a Dangerous World: A New Political Risk Index
10. González Cano, J. 1996. *Armonización Tributaria del Mercosur. Buenos Aires: Instituto Universitario de Finanzas Públicas Argentinas.*
11. Government of Tanzania, Income Tax Act 2004
12. Government of Tanzania, Value Added Tax Act 2006

13. Hamada J., Haugerudbraaten H., Hickman A., Khaykin I. (2004), *Country and Political Risk. Practical Insights for Global Finances*, S. Wilkins, Risk Books
14. Harry M. Kitlya (2011) Tax Administrative Reforms in Tanzania-Experiences and Challenges-Conference Paper on Revenue Mobilization in Developing countries-IFM Fiscal Affair-Washington D.C
15. International Monetary Fund, 2005 "International Financial Statistic March 2005
16. Investment Promotion Act no. 6 of 2004 Sessional paper No. 2 of 19 on small Enterprise and Jua Kali Development in Kenya.
17. Jackson, B. R., & Million, V. C. (1986). Tax compliance research: Findings, problems, and prospects. *Journal of Accounting Literature*, 5 (1), 25-65.
18. Jonathan Di John (2006): The political Economy of Taxation and Tax reforms in developing countries. United Nations University, Research paper No 76, pp 1-27
19. Kasaro and Kiria (2009), Tax Incentives. *The Accountant. Journal of the National board of Accounts and Auditors Tanzania, Volume 24 Issue*
20. Kichler, E., E. Hoelzl & I. Wahl 2008. Enforced versus voluntary tax compliance: The "slippery slope" framework. Journal of Economic Psychology, 29, 210-225.
21. Krugman, Paul (1979). "A model of Balance of Payments Crises." Journal of Money, Credit, and Banking, 11, 311-25.
22. Lekinyi N. Mollel (2009), *Impact of Debt Relief on Fiscal Allocation to Priority Social Sectors and Response of Social Indicators in the HIPCS: A Case study of Tanzania*
23. Lekinyi N. Mollel (2009), *private sector External Debt Management Tanzania, Paper presented at sensitization seminar on commercial banks on the importance of private sector external debt.*
24. Levin, J. (2009) Taxation in Tanzania – Revenue Performances and Incidents Country Economic Report 2005, Sida, Helniski.
25. Lise Rakner and Sari Gloppen (2002). Tax Reforms and Democratic Accountability in Sub- Sahara Africa

26. Ministry of Finance (2010), Special Incentives for Manufacturers and Exporters Republic of Namibia Publication
27. Mistry, PS, 1996. *Regional Integration Arrangements in Economic Development, Panacea or Pitfall* FONDAD, The Hague
28. Odd H. Fjeldstad L (2003) Taxation and tax reforms in developing countries Illustration from Sub-Saharan Africa; Chr. Michelsen Institute Development Studies and Human Rights
29. Palil, M. R. (2010). *Tax knowledge and tax compliance determinants in self-assessment system in Malaysia.* University of Birmingham.
30. Richupan, S. 1987. Determination of income tax evasion: Role of tax rates, shape of taxs schedules and other factors. In: Gandhi, V. P. (ed.). International Monetary Fund.
31. Schiff, M and LA Winters, 2003. Regional Integration and Development. World Bank, DC.
32. Steinmo, Sven, 1993. Taxation and Democracy: Swedish, British, and American Approaches to Financing the Modern State (New Haven: Yale University Press)
33. Shome P. (2004) Tax Administration and the Small Taxpayer IMF Policy Discussion Paper PDP/04/2Fiscal Affairs Department
34. Snavely, K. (1990) Governmental policies to reduce tax evasion: coerced behavior versus services and values development. *Policy Science*, 23, 57-72
35. Tanzania Economic Survey 2009; Ministry of finance and Economic Affairs KIATU
36. Tanzania Investment Act 1997
37. Tayler T. R. 2006. Psychological perspectives on Legitimacy and legitimation. *Annual Review of Psychology*, 57, 375-400.
38. Teunissen, JJ, 1996. Regionalism and the Global Economy, The Case of Africa. FONDAD, The Hague.
39. The income Tax Act (Cap 470), Laws of Kenya. Government Printer
40. The Land Act and the Village Land Act 1999
41. Thirlwall, A. P. and M. N. Hussain, 1982 "The Balance of Payments Constraints, Capital flow and Growth Rate Differences between

Developing Countries." Oxford Economic Papers, Vol. 10, page 498-509
42. UNACTAD (2002), Investment policy review (Tanzania)
43. UNCTAD (2000), Tax incentives and Foreign Direct Investment, A Global Survey, Geneva, Swiss.
44. Value Added Tax (Cap 476), Laws of Kenya. Government Printer
45. World Bank (2000). Trade Blocs. A World Bank Policy Research Report. Oxford University Press, New York.
46. World Bank, 2000. *Accelerating Integration in West Africa: A Discussion Paper, World Bank, 2000*

About the Author

Prof Dr Lucky Yona is a Director of Research and Publication at ESAMI (Eastern and Southern African Management Institute). He holds a Doctorate of Business Administration (DBA), Master's Degree in Business Administration (MBA) and Masters of Philosophy (MPHIL) from Maastricht, Bachelor of commerce (BCOM) and Bachelor of Theology (B.Th.). He is also a Certified Public Accountant (CPA). Presently he is finalizing his PHD (Doctor of Philosophy) degree with Euraka University (Switzerland). Lucky is an experienced Consultant and International Trainer. He has also published various books in the area of finance and accounting and numerous papers in International Peer Reviewed Journals. Prior to joining ESAMI he worked with various reputable institutions and companies in different senior capacities. He was previously the Financial Administrator (AMREF), Business Manager (International School of Moshi), College Bursar (Kilimanjaro Christian Medical College) and Chief Accountant (Iscor Mining). He has also taught at the Nyegezi Social Training Institute (Now St Augustine University in Tanzania). Lucky teaches the MBA courses at ESAMI Business School and specializes teaching Financial Accounting, Corporate Finance and International Finance.

www.ingramcontent.com/pod-product-compliance
Lightning Source LLC
Chambersburg PA
CBHW021541200526
45163CB00014B/441